Nepal, 2019.

# FATALISM AND DEVELOPMENT

## NEPAL'S STRUGG

# FATALISM AND DEVELOPMENT

## NEPAL'S STRUGGLE FOR MODERNIZATION

Dor Bahadur Bista

Orient BlackSwan

**FATALISM AND DEVELOPMENT**
Nepal's Struggle for Modernization

**ORIENT BLACKSWAN PRIVATE LIMITED**

*Registered Office*
3-6-752 Himayatnagar, Hyderabad 500 029, Telangana, India
E-mail : centraloffice@orientblackswan.com

*Other Offices*
Bengaluru, Bhopal, Chennai, Guwahati,
Hyderabad, Jaipur, Kolkata, Lucknow, Mumbai,
New Delhi, Noida, Patna, Vijaywada



First Published 1991 in hardback
First Paperback Edition 2008
Reprinted 2008, 2011, 2015, 2016

ISBN : 978 81 250 3460 5

*Lasertypeset by*
Vishnu Datagraphics
Kolkata

*Printed by*
Commercial Press Service
Kolkata - 700 012

*Published by*
Orient Blackswan Private Limited
17, Chittaranjan Avenue, Kolkata - 700 072
E-mail : kolkata@orientblackswan.com

Dedicated to the People of Nepal

# CONTENTS

# PREFACE

The typescript of this book was completed in the summer of 1989 and was submitted for publication immediately afterwards. The period between then and now has seen some remarkable changes in the political system of the country. The chapter on 'Politics and Government' has been updated accordingly, but the rest of the book has been left as it was.

This book deals mainly with the socio-cultural aspects and the value system of the Nepali society which still remains as has been described in the following pages. With the introduction of the liberal and democratic multi-party political system possibilities have been opened up for the desired changes in the social structure. We can be optimistic about the future, but it is yet to be seen.

June 1990 Dor Bahadur Bista

If there are no trees, there will be no water whenever one looks for it. The watering places will become dry. If forests are cut down, there will be avalanches. If there are many avalanches, there will be great accidents. Accidents also destroy the fields. Without forests, the householder's work can not be accomplished. Therefore, he who cuts down the forest near a watering place will be fined five rupees.

*Fourteenth Edict of King Ram Shah (1606-1636)*

I have faith in the future, and I hope that the day will come when all will see clearly what now only a few suspect.

*Alexis Tocqueville*

# ACKNOWLEDGEMENTS

The people of Nepal have helped create this book. I saw them invariably tied to their traditional structures and values of the past while struggling to enter into new horizons of the future. The dynamics of struggle, conflict, contradiction and trauma were real and obvious. I would like to express my gratitude towards all those who thus provided the theme for the book.

Devraj Dahal, Krishna Bahadur Bhattachan, Indra Basnyat, John C. Cool, Joseph Elder, Carl Coon Jr., James Fisher, my son Keshar and daughter Asha read the manuscript at the earlier stages of its growth and gave valuable advice for its improvement. Sarah Tisch and Wendy Fillipitch helped edit the earlier version. My son Hikmat and Barry K. Barnes took care of all the technicalities and organized the manuscript for publication. Colleagues at Tribhuvan University and the graduate students at the Department of Sociology-Anthropology gave opportunities to discuss some of my ideas with them.

The Toyota Foundation and the Ford Foundation provided financial grants for research and writing. The Center for Nepal and Asian Studies (CNAS) and the then Executive Director, Khadga Bikram Shah; and the International Center for Integrated Mountain Development (ICIMOD) and the then Director, Colin Rosser gave technical and administrative support.

Towards the final stages of the work a British Council Fellowship gave me an opportunity to visit Cambridge University for three months where I received advice on the manuscript from Ernest Gellner; Alan Macfarlane and Sarah Harrison provided liberal hospitality in addition to the advice for improvement of the manuscript and helped edit the final version later on when they were on a visit to Nepal. The Ford

Foundation provided an additional grant for residence at the Center for South and Southeast Asian Studies at the University of California, Berkeley, for six months where I enjoyed both generous hospitality and advice for improvement of the text from Leo E. Rose. I am deeply indebted to all of them.

I have made use of information and ideas presented in many published works as well as those expressed formally or informally by many academic people, and yet I am alone responsible for expressing them in my own style and arriving at my own conclusions.

I consider this work only as a beginning for the purpose I have stated. Better ones are sure to come later.

# INTRODUCTION

This work examines aspects of cultural and social organization of Nepali society, as they have an effect on Nepal's development. Nepal remained a medieval society until 1950, when the Rana prime ministers, who had been effective rulers of the country for over a century, were overthrown and replaced by a democratic government, operating under the scrutiny of an actively interested and ultimately powerful monarch. The Ranas had fostered policies of nepotism and isolationism, perpetuating a social stagnation that had started in the preceding era. The new government has had as one of its primary goals the guided revitalization of the country and its introduction into the global community as a fully functioning economic member. But the attempts at development have met with mixed success.

Certain elements of Nepali society have become impatient with what is seen as a slow rate of development, and the increasing economic disparity among different sections of the people. This has led to various forms of dissatisfaction. Material benefits accrued as a result of economic change have been, in part, deflected to privileged classes through processes of distribution outside normal market activities. Accommodations have been made in the structure of Nepali society, but there are indications that these structural changes may actually interfere with the long term adjustment of Nepali society to the exigencies of change, and this is largely due to the prevalent attitude and the predominant value system of the Nepali society at the elite level.

This work specifically attempts to isolate key factors in Nepali society that are retarding and diminishing its effort to develop. Nepal is a heteronomous society with a complex ethnic mix, overlaid by disparities in social and economic opportunity. The human element in Nepal is diverse and its contribution in defining the development potential of Nepal is complex. Within its diversity are some potentially valuable resources. In various areas of Nepal may be found the social qualities that, with the correct external facilitation, may generate and sustain the kind of progress envisioned by national planners. These include a strong commitment to productive labour, a high capacity for endurance, efficient cooperative organizational styles, and a high adaptive propensity at individual and social levels. In the past, Nepalis have been known as effective merchants and craftsmen. But these characteristics are not shared by all Nepalis, nor are they equally distributed across the nation. Rather they characterize discrete groups within Nepali society and currently these particular groups are not socially placed where these characteristics may be advantageously utilized.

The current nature of Nepali society is such that the groups with positive elements of value systems in their social and collective practices are increasingly excluded from the mainstream of society and their values are endangered as another, essentially alien, culture becomes more pervasive. This other culture, the culture of fatalism, includes values and institutions that are inherently in conflict with development. In Nepal, the culture of fatalism devalues the concept of productivity. The productive sector of the society is increasingly getting discouraged in the proportion that the fatalistic culture is being encouraged and propagated, while its proponents are gaining ascendancy. Most development and the rising standard of living has been attained through the heavy infusion of external aid. The beneficiaries have not always been those who actually contribute to growth and production. But the irony is that those who enjoy the benefits continue to be increasingly unhappy and ask for more without contributing to the process of development.

While these disparate and inherently conflicting value systems do have connections with specific ethnic groups within Nepal, the inherent conflict should not be seen as an ethnic one. Ethnic conflict is not currently a problem for Nepal. The inherent conflict in Nepali society betrays a tension in social structure whose definition should be made in terms of both class and caste. Caste is an appealing target for westernized investigators and has been singled out as being at the base of many of Nepal's developmental difficulties. But issues of caste are not as simple as they have been generally regarded to be. This is because in Nepal there is no rigorous caste system as is frequently believed. Though the concept of caste was not unknown to Nepal even in ancient days, it has only started to become pervasive in the last century. It varies greatly from the orthodox caste societies found elsewhere. In some circumstances pollution is attached to certain elements within the social structure, the structure is typically ascriptive, and caste has a limited acceptance to the extent that it has been useful in consolidating class privileges. Any rigidities associated with an ascriptive system will have an adverse effect on development and Nepal suffers from these problems. These will be considered here, but not in isolation. Issues of caste are merely elements of a cultural system that has even more insidious effects on Nepali society through certain key elements of its central values. These values have had effects on both the individual and the social level.

Religion has always been a central feature of Nepali life but Nepal has never been plagued by any form of religious fanaticism. On the contrary, Nepalis love colourful rituals of all kinds and have welcomed a variety of religious traditions. Prominent are Shamanism, Shaivism, Buddhism, Tantrism, and Vaisnavism. It is only the class system legitimized by the caste system with its attendant adverse cultural elements that will be addressed here. Although the term Bahunism (Brahmanism) has been used frequently to mean the syndrome of cultural configurations along with the principles of caste system introduced by the Brahmans arriving in the Kathmandu Valley and in the Karnali basin during the medieval period, it does not imply that it has anything to do with the bulk of the Nepali population bearing Bahun family names today. In fact, many people from this background are actually busy fighting the syndrome, while many people from a non-Bahun background are busily engaged in pushing the various forms of the archaic ideology inherent in the stratified caste system. Besides, the people who imposed the system upon the Nepali society were not the Bahuns. They could not have done it by themselves as they were weak, dependent immigrants at the time. It was the local ruling elite who were responsible for doing this by applying the Bahunistic principles for further entrenchment of their own class status.

The most important effect of this has been the absolute belief in fatalism: that one has no personal control over one's life circumstances, which are determined through a divine or powerful external agency. This deep belief in fatalism has had a devastating effect on the work ethic and achievement motivation, and through these on the Nepali response to development. It has consequences on the sense of time, and in particular such things as the concept of planning, orientation to the future, sense of causality, human dignity and punctuality.

Fatalism is highly connected to various forms of dependency, which may be part of a more basic Nepali cultural system. Besides its connections with fatalism, Nepali dependency can be seen in a mature form in the harmonious cooperative social behaviour within indigenous groups. Nepalis are not strong individualists, as are Americans for example, but are what some call collectivists. Collectivism in itself is not necessarily an impediment to development, as evident in the critical role it has played in the Japanese success and in the smooth progress of the Kathmandu Valley society until the introduction of the stratified caste system during the medieval period.

In Nepal, today, collectivism manifests in a particular social institution of much importance known as *afno manchhe* (one's own people). Afno manchhe has the potential of being constructively used as a natural form of social organization within Nepal, but it can also be readily subverted to negative ends. In particular it encourages problems of inclusion-exclusion, as group members gain particular privileges. Being a part of the outer circle it can impede cooperative action. Difficulties also arise when membership in a desired circle of afno manchhe can be purchased only through traded privileges. With afno manchhe one finds exclusionary tendencies, factionalism, failures in cooperation, and corruption in various forms leading to malfunctioning of development administration and dissatisfaction at every level.

Dependency and fatalism combined together exacerbate the tendency to impede development. An example can be found in the practice of *chakari*. The origin of chakari (sycophancy) lies in religious ritual practices of obeisance, which was extended to the governing classes and then to all in certain positions of power. As a social activity, its most common form is in simply being close to or in the presence of the person whose favour is desired. Instead of efficient fulfilment of duties and obligations, persistence in chakari is seen as merit, and with enough merit favours may be granted. It is a passive form of instrumental behaviour whose object is to demonstrate dependency, with the aim of eventually eliciting the favour of the person depended upon.

Chakari behaviour is often the lifetime occupation of the adult, though the rewards can be great. By practising chakari over several generations a particular family may even be able to raise its class or caste status. Chakari has to be nourished and requires persistence. The strategy of chakari and the concept of productivity in those who practise it are alien to modern economic thought and systems, and can in no way support genuine development. Chakari is an indication that Nepal not only needs to learn new things in order to progress, but must also unlearn old things. Chakari may not be easy to eradicate, but it needs to be purged if economic success is to be a reality in Nepal.

Fatalism and dependency may allow perversion of developmental aid. In its most blatant form this perversion manifests itself in the expectation of foreign aid as a divinely instigated redistribution.The peculiar geo-political situation of Nepal has helped its elites to develop an attitude of acceptance and of adaptation to any influence from outside. On the other hand a sense of equanimity has also provided a measure of resilience which has helped Nepal maintain its independent and sovereign status. Ironically, the same background was congenial for the infusion of a fatalistic principle that conditions the attitude towards foreign aid today. In the present context aid becomes merely something that is justly due to Nepal and not a resource that is meant to be considered seriously and used productively.

This has also had its effects on education. Scholarship in the Sanskritic tradition is associated with privilege and never with labour. Education is traditionally the prerogative of the upper classes: to be educated is a powerful symbol of status.

Education is not perceived as a means of acquiring skills that can be used productively to secure economic prosperity but is seen as an end in itself which once achieved signifies higher status, and in association with which the privileges of status are expected automatically. As educational opportunities increase and become accessible to lower classes, the educated lower class use education as a means to rapid social advancement, but the traditional route is used. Acquisition of education is the perceived acquisition of status and there is an expectation that it will be immediately associated with privilege. To become educated is to be effectively removed from the workforce. Within such an atmosphere a genuinely productive professional workforce can never be developed and professional activities must continue to be performed by the untrained. Those that do have a productive orientation towards education, and have gone ahead to acquire technical and professional skills with the intention of using these to improve their circumstance and those of others around them, are usually not recognized and are not considered as models. There is, then, a cluster of cultural elements, including but extending beyond that of caste, that play a very important negative role in Nepal's attempt at change. These cultural elements are connected particularly with fatalistic hierarchy, which has a following within a restricted but critically important sector of Nepali society. Much of this book will concentrate on this sector as it has played and continues to play the central role in the history of Nepal. Outside of the Kathmandu Valley the situation changes. There we are more likely to find many of the positive cultural traits among the many ethnic groups currently outside the ambit of fatalistic and ascriptive models. They remain the great hope of Nepal but still there is danger. Fatalistic hierarchy is not an antiquated nor an exhausted cultural force. As a real factor it is relatively new to Nepal and it is currently spreading. All ethnic groups are being affected by it.

This book is based on observations made over thirty years on Nepal's attempt to develop and respond to change. It grows out of my previous ethnographic work, which represented a characterization of the diverse ethnic traditions within Nepal (Bista, 1967). Vast changes of various kinds have occurred since then. Therefore this work concentrates on the cultural system, the hub of which is within the national centre in the Kathmandu Valley, although I have frequently made references to areas outside the valley. While it is the work of an anthropologist, it is also the work of a student of the Nepali society and has developed from an appreciation of social process within Nepal.

This book struggles to present the Nepali perception of social process. It is a struggle because Nepal is such a complex cultural conglomeration seeking perpetually to accommodate, if not synthesize, its diverse discrete parts. Nepali society is heteronomous and is in a constant flux. This makes the process of analytic generalization difficult and subject to even more qualification than is normally the case. Nonetheless, I believe my generalizations to be warranted with the caution that the book is centred on the cultural systems of the major groups of the high caste Hindus. But generalization is the only way with which we can learn anything about the complex society such as that of Nepal. Edmund Leach suggested that, 'Generalization is inductive, it consists in perceiving possible general laws in the circumstances of special cases; it is guesswork, a gamble, you may be wrong or you may be right, but if you happen to be right you have learned something altogether new'.(Leach, 1966).

I also believe that an intracultural approach to the study of Hindu society permits valid levels of generalization, even while such societies are being subjected to change and therefore going through a period of disorder (Burghart, 1983).

Some readers may find fault with the generalizations as they will have had their own personal experiences and will be aware of exceptions that do not conform to the picture I have presented here. But to insist on exceptions to prove the generalizations wrong would suggest that Nepali society is beyond the reach of a systematic study under any discipline in the social sciences; and by inference, beyond the possibility of guided correction, change and development.

While there are many critics of Nepal from among the dominant groups, the form of their criticism, though embellished with different dressings, is essentially of the same ilk and remains encumbered with a parochial perspective. Educated members of this group may be aware of the plight of Nepal and the need for social change but rarely do they recognise how their own particular culture has contributed to these impoverished circumstances. Some members of the dominant high caste group will be shocked by assertions that I will make; not only as a defensive reaction, but because very few among them have ever learnt to question the negative impact of their own life style and their own attitude on Nepali society. Typically, a great majority of the critics like to focus on politico-economic aspects of the society for every evil of Nepal. Rarely do they look into the socio-cultural and religious values they have imposed upon the national society. This phenomenon has not been as rigorously dissected so far, as attempted here, and many of these ideas therefore will be new to them. I am aware that I have started on an extremely difficult journey of conducting a critical examination of my own society. The precarious job of walking on a thin edge, frequently changing sides from being an object to be studied to being an outsider who studies at the same time has, by no means, been easy.

Attempts by most scholars to understand and then represent Nepali society, especially the dynamics of the predominant Nepali culture, have typically been burdened by a theoretical framework, used for the study of social stratification, developed by a western mentality that attempts to represent Hindu caste society either based on the Indian model or as a periphery of the western centres of industrial capitalism and imperialism(Blaikie et al, 1980). Nepal is not like India. This is a critical point. And an overemphasis on the structural qualities of caste often simply obscures more critical issues concerning value systems. In a way, this book denies the statement made by Sylvain Levi in the beginning of the century that Nepal is India in the making (*le Nepal c'est l'Inde qui se fait*). Instead it asserts that Nepal's problems follow from certain attempts at the Indianization of its culture.

Nepal's strengths have always been in the indigenous qualities of its various ethnic groups. The attempt to follow the Indian model has often overwhelmed and suppressed these qualities, substituting them with something which is incongruent with its own culture and ultimately defeating progressive adaptation and change. Indian culture and civilization have made positive contribution to the development of Nepal from the earliest times to the present in the fields of fine arts, music, literature, architecture, metal and woodcrafts and in the skills of business management and commerce. They can do so in future and we should be open to them, but what Nepal takes from India, or any other culture, needs to be scrutinized and its negative elements purged. Hindu caste culture contains negative elements which need to be identified, localized and, if possible, exorcized.

What we will examine critically is the negative influence of caste culture which was first felt in Nepal during the sixteenth century and became all pervasive during the middle of the nineteenth. It was manifested in an extremely individualized and defensive form of self-preservation as Bahunism, mainly as a reaction against the ruthless carnage carried out by the Moghuls during this period. As a result some people in Nepal remain emotionally tied and loyal to Indian religio-cultural connections even while they are politically openly anti-Indian. Such people feel politically threatened by India and culturally by the West.

This book is divided into eight distinct chapters. The first chapter provides general information on Nepal, including a brief regional description, its ethnic heritage and an overview of Nepalese history. The second chapter focuses on Nepal's social organization, with a more in-depth consideration of the role of religion and caste in Nepali society, the relations between caste and class, ethnic groupings, kinship structures and gender relations. The third chapter looks at family and socialization practices, as a prelude to the following chapter which concentrates on psycho-social factors, focusing on fatalism, temporal orientation, dependency, collectivism, and achievement motivation. This chapter also includes an elaboration of afno manchhe, which is a particular manifestation of collectivism, and chakari, which is considered in the context of Nepali cognition of causality, instrumentality, and dependency. The fifth and sixth chapters consider two sets of institutions that must play a critical role in Nepal's development, the political and the educational. In these chapters a general review of the political and educational systems is presented and their dynamics considered in the light of the cultural peculiarities elucidated in the previous two chapters. The seventh chapter details Nepali perspectives on foreign aid and describes practices in the formulation and distribution of foreign aid that are failing to achieve their ends in the Nepali context. The final chapter is a general discussion on the potential contribution of the various ethnic groups in Nepal to development, and considers, briefly the issue of creating a national identity.

CHAPTER ONE

# GENERAL BACKGROUND

Nepal embraces one of the most diverse climatic ranges and physical environments of the world within a short span of 26°22′ and 33°27′ of the northern latitude. In the approximately 100 miles between the Gangetic plain and the Tibetan plateau, there are at least seven distinct geographic zones in Nepal: the plains (Terai), the Siwalik range and the Mahabharata range, which generally run parallel, though sometimes merge with the Siwalik, creating a chain of valleys which are called Bhitri Madhes (Inner Terai), a mid-montane area between the first set of mountain ranges and the Himalayas, the Himalaya range itself, and the high mountain valleys of the Inner Himalaya. Permanent settlements are found in a wide variety of ecological niches, from central Asian alpine valleys at an altitude of 14,000 ft. above sea level to depressions in the South Asian plains with an altitude of less than 200 ft. above sea level. Unlike the plains, the Himalayas and their foothills do not provide many areas which can sustain a permanent settlement for a sizeable population anywhere outside of Kathmandu Valley. The Kathmandu Valley, situated at an average altitude of 1,500 meters above sea level in the mid-montane area, has a temperate climate and is the only place in the entire Himalaya which is relatively flat and endowed with fertile soil.

The large majority of people live in hamlets scattered across the country. Besides the three ancient cities within Kathmandu Valley, there are a few small urbanized areas which have developed within the last fifty years. Until recently, migration throughout Nepal was easy as there was enough fallow land for newcomers or there were people who owned large tracts of land and needed landless people to work for them. Landowners encouraged migrant workers to settle permanently on their land and work in share-cropping arrangements. As a result, though there are certain areas of Nepal that are strongly associated with particular ethnic groups, there is also an extensive scattering of Nepal's different ethnic groups across its entire length and breadth. Since land has become scarce, the central authorities have taken the initiative to resettle people in a planned manner in the Terai.

In ancient times, the Terai was the location of several significant kingdoms and must have supported a sizeable population. Following socio-political upheavals, including Islamic invasions in the eleventh, fourteenth and sixteenth centuries, the whole Terai suffered from major population declines, which was followed by extensive natural reforestation of the area. During the nineteenth century, there was a population-drift back into the Terai with an accompanying development of its agricultural capacity. Consequently, the Terai became known as the 'breadbasket of Nepal'. The geography of the Terai has also, more recently, favoured the development of an extensive system of roads. This, combined with its proximity to the Indian railhead and the current plentiful supply of labour, has also encouraged Nepali industry to concentrate and develop in the Terai, though some industry has developed in the Kathmandu Valley. Essentially, then, the Terai is the location of Nepal's agricultural wealth as well as her industrial capacity; the hill and mountain regions are dependent on tourism, exploitation of water resources for energy and, otherwise, operate on a simple subsistence level.

Traditionally, the regions of Nepal were identified by the names of its various major ethnic communities (see figure 1). For instance, the eastern hills beyond Sunkosi were called the Kirat Pradesh (Kirat region). This area was divided into three subregions whose designations were assigned on the basis of their proximity to the Kathmandu Valley: the area from Sunkosi river to the Likhu was called the Wollo Kirat (near Kirat); the area between the Likhu and the Arun was called Manjh Kirat (middle Kirat); and the land stretching east of the Arun to the Indian border was called the Pallo Kirat (far Kirat). Similarly, the regions in the west of the valley, all the way to the Kali Gandaki was traditionally known as the Gandaki Pradesh. The area west of this, to the Karnali, was called Magarant (region of the Magars), and the region along the Karnali and beyond was called Khasaan (Land of the Khas).

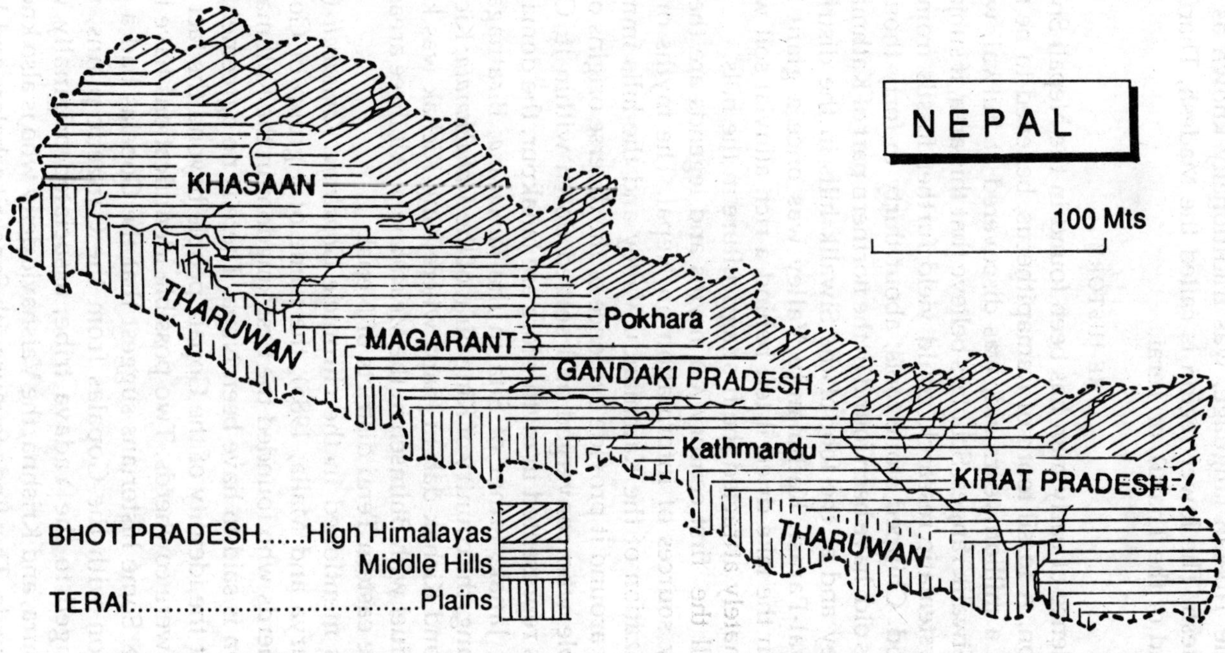


Figure 1. The traditional ethnic-based regional areas of Nepal

The high-altitude area, inhabited by people speaking dialects of the Tibetan language, was traditionally known as Bhot Pradesh. The lower region is called the Madesh, Tharuwan (Land of the Tharu), or Terai.

## PRE-HISTORY

Evidence of early man has been found in the Nepali Siwalik region. A fossil tooth of Ramapithecus, believed to be more than a million years old, was discovered at Butwal, within the Siwalik ranges. Scholars believe that this area, if subjected to systematic research, could yield further fossils from this period. Chipped stone tools, about thirty to forty thousand years old, have been found in the northern part of Kathmandu Valley and at the foot of the Siwalik hills in the district of Nawal-Parasi. Kathmandu Valley was once a giant lake. When the lake dried it left behind a rich alluvial soil which ultimately attracted the first agriculture in the hills.

Till the first century A.D. myths and legends are the primary sources of information on Nepal. The myths on the civilization of the Kathmandu Valley and the hills immediately around it provide evidence of the diverse origins of the people who converged and settled down within it. Other areas represented in mythic lore are Janakpur, the domain of King Janak, father of Sita in the *Ramayana*; Biratnagar in Morang, the country of King Birat of the *Mahabharata*; Kichakban and Kichak-dah in Jhapa where King Kichak was killed in a duel with Bhimsen in the *Mahabharata*. All three areas are in the eastern Terai districts of Nepal.

As mentioned in the chronicle *Gopalraja Vamsavali* (Vajracharya and Malla, 1985), the name of a group of Gopala cowherds who founded the first kingdom in the Kathmandu region is said to have been Nepa. There is no agreement yet about the identity of the Gopala people beyond the fact that they were cowherds. Two possible identifications have been made. Some historians suggest that the Gopalas had a connection with the Gopalas from the Gangetic plains, who belonged to the Yadava tribe, associated originally with Mathura, and Kṛishna, the Vaisnavic deity who is also known as Gopala. This finds favour with Sanskrit scholars and Vaisnav pundits within Nepal. Others suggest that these early settlers were called Gopala simply because they were pastoral nomads and not because they descended from the Gopalas of the plains (Panta, 1987: 213). Gopala is a Sanskrit word in which 'go' means cow, and 'pala' means herder or keeper. The Gopalas who founded the first settlements in the Kathmandu Valley used a more primitive agricultural technology than that of the relatively advanced agriculturalists from the plains. The first attempts at agriculture in the valley seem more like the work of pastoral peoples such as the Kirat and the Khas (Bista, 1982).

Although today the Kirats are associated particularly with the hilly regions east of the Kathmandu Valley, in the ancient period the Kirat regions extended into the western hills as well. They are Mongoloids and spoke a Tibeto-Burmese language, though their descendants have now mixed with other racial groups. The Kirats are thought to have moved from the east, with their domesticated pigs and buffaloes, along the lower hills through warm, humid, and forested areas, where they practised a shifting cultivation.

The Khas were pastoralists, associated particularly with the western hills of Nepal, and had connections with west Central Asia. They speak an Indo-Aryan language and appear to have arrived with their cattle, goats and sheep in the western reaches of Nepal around the beginning of the first millenium B.C. Their cultivation was restricted to growing barley, millet, and sesame. Evidence suggests that when the Khas met the Kirat they were able to assert their dominance over them and established Khas rule in the western hills, as well as in the Kathmandu Valley. Though this evidence is far from conclusive, it seems reasonable to assume that the nomadic-pastoralist Khas are the gopalas or cow-herders of tradition.

The Khas learnt much from the Kirat, including dry rice cultivation and a sedentary agricultural lifestyle. Their new circumstances facilitated the development of a social order with a more centralized economic and political organization. The Gopala people are believed to have founded their capital in Matatirtha, at the western end of the Kathmandu Valley, when they established the first state of Nepal (see figure 2). They still live there today. The Kirat, however, formed the bulk of the population and, with time, established their own dominance and their capital of Gokarna in the eastern Kathmandu Valley and through the eastern regions of what is now

Figure 2. The earliest mentioned places of Nepal

modern Nepal. Khas dominance was to continue in the western regions throughout the historical period. The new Kirat state, established sometime during the early first millenium B.C., was to last for a thousand years. Most of the names of the places, rivers, deities and spirits of the ancient period have their origins in the Tibeto-Burmese Kirat or the Indo-Iranian Khas languages (Malla, 1981) suggesting the limited influence of Gangetic society in the south at this time.

The Kirat descendants include all Indo-Mongolian people speaking various Tibeto-Burmese dialects as their mother tongue, the principal of which are the Rai, Limbu, Yakha, Sunuwar, Jirel, Hayu, Gurung, Magar, Thakali, Thami, and Chepang in the hills, and the Tharu, Danuwar, Bote Majhi, Dhimal, Meche, Koche in the plains (see figure 3). The earliest Newar of Kathmandu are also thought to belong to this general group. Beside the Kirat and Khas groups, there are others, such as the Dhangads, who speak a Dravidian language and appear to have Dravidian characteristics. Also, some of the groups speaking Tibeto-Burmese dialects have predominantly Dravidian physical characteristics, such as the Raute. As previously mentioned, there has been much migration within Nepal, resulting in intermingling of the various racial groups.

Despite the migration of groups from the Gangetic plains into the Nepali region, the Kirat have been able to maintain a distinct cultural identity, especially in the Kathmandu Valley region, and the Newar people continue to evolve their own culture, language, and literature. This perpetuation of Kirat culture would have been possible if the rate of migration of latecomers into the Kathmandu region, particularly from the south, was slight, since the valley is very small and its population was never very dense at any time in the past. If a sizeable migrant group had arrived from the plains, Nepali society would have easily been overwhelmed and Sanskritized, and this was never done.

## ANCIENT HISTORY

There are several scattered references to Nepal in Indian literature prior to the Common Era. The Puranas mention that the Kirat king, Yelambar, participated in the battle of Mahabharata, and make reference to Shiva as the god of the Kirat.

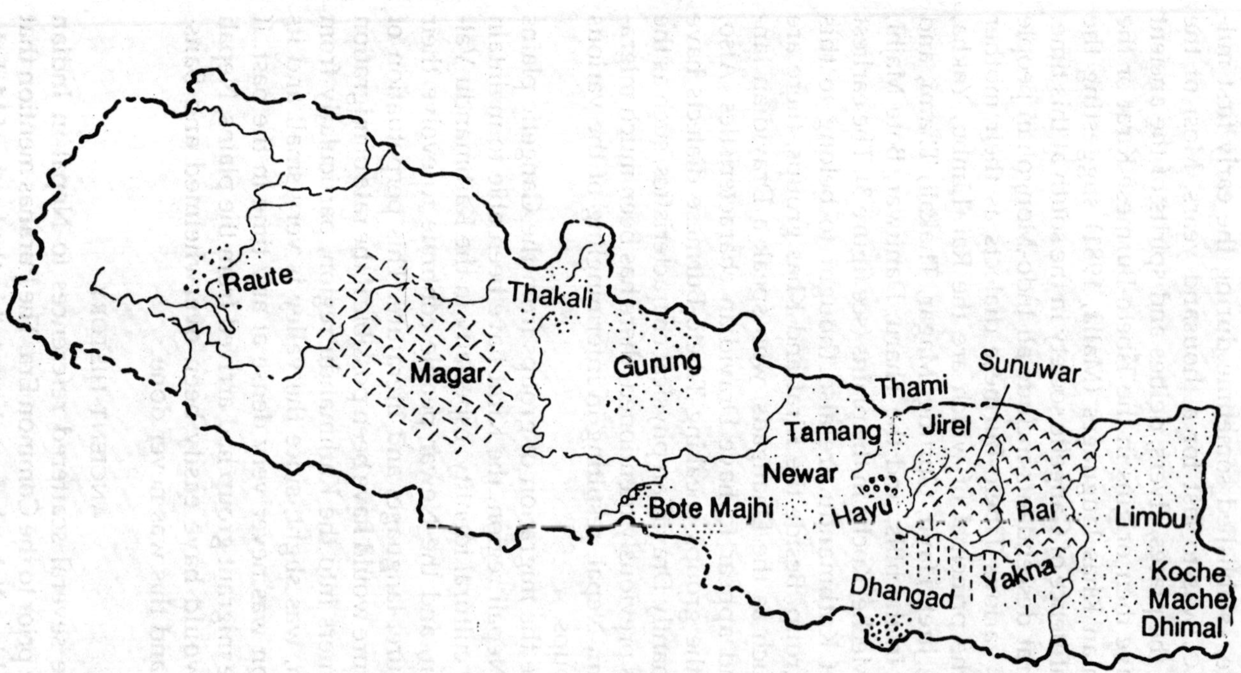


Figure 3. Major Kirat groups and their regional centres

Nepal is also mentioned in the *Atharvaparisista, Kurmavibhaga*, dating from around the eighth to the sixth century B.C. In this work, Nepal takes its place among the celebrated nations of the time, such as Kamarupa (Assam), Videha (North Bihar), Udambara (Punjab), and Avanti (Madhyabharat). Another reference is made in the text of Kautilya's *Arthashastra* (fourth century B.C.) in relation to the making and exportation of a special woollen material called Bhingishi, a shawl of good quality, as well as musk, gold, silver, elephants, and horses, which Nepal traded with India (Sharma, 1967). An ancient name for Matatirtha is Kishipirhi, which means Elephant Centre, suggesting that there was a significant population of elephants in the Kathmandu Valley at that time. Mostly, though, elephants would have been captured in the Terai regions, while the musk, gold, silver, and short-legged mountain ponies came from the high Himalayas and from the Tibetan regions, and other horses from the lands of the Khas pastoralists in the west. This list of early exported materials is important because it suggests a fairly widespread exploitation of resources from diverse geographical regions, and a very early connection with the Tibetan plateau.

The Terai has something of an independent history in ancient times, although the kingdoms which arose there have connections both with the Gangetic plains and the Nepali hills. Lumbini, Kapilavastu, and Devdah were all important sites in the west, and Janakpur was important in the east. Kapilavastu was an important early Buddhist centre associated with Gautama. These early kingdoms were decimated by disease and largely reforested until Simaraungarh was founded near the former site of Janakpur. Simaraungarh was later destroyed by the Moslems in the fourteenth century and the region was again naturally reforested.

The cultures of the northern Gangetic plains have greatly influenced Nepal in every respect from pre-historic days. There may have been early arrivals from these plains, including the Buddhist Sakyas, the Koliya, the Malla, and sometime later the Licchavis and Guptas. Others have more recently suggested that some of these Nepali dynasties may have been indigenous to Nepal, with borrowed 'pedigrees' from the plains to suggest a connection with prominent and ancient ruling families there. The advent of each of these dynasties parallels the further introduction of aspects of Indian culture. But Nepal has always retained her own identity and has integrated these alien cultural intrusions into something uniquely Nepali.

The Sakyas are associated with the introduction of Mahayana Buddhism to Nepal and are credited with the creation of the Buddhist landmarks which mark the beginning of Nepal's cultural history. They were followed by the Licchavis and Guptas. Of all the ancient people of the valley, the best documented, and, therefore, better known to us, are the Licchavis, though from the first century to the tenth century power oscillated between the Licchavis and the Guptas. The Licchavis were an ancient and significant family in Indian history on the Gangetic plains, first appearing in the sixth and seventh centuries B.C. They ruled at Vaishali, in India, during the early Buddhist period, were related to the rulers of Magadha, and, much later, in the fourth century, were related to the Indian Guptas through Samudragupta, whose mother was said to be a Licchavi queen. The Nepali Guptas were responsible for introducing Vaisnavic culture, around the fourth century, installing the Narayana (Vishnu) shrines at the four corners of the valley.

Despite their alleged Indian background, administrative terminologies and place names of the early Licchavi period are mainly in non-Sanskritic languages, which demonstrates the continuation of Kirat cultural primacy in the hills and in the Kathmandu Valley (Regmi, 1969: 357-8). There was one significant cultural introduction within this period, however, which involved an element of social organization that is essentially alien to the Kirat cultural system. This was the varna or caste system introduced, in part, by the Guptas.[1] Nepali Shaivism was not connected to the varna system, and Buddhism was essentially opposed to the concept of caste, so that it was only with the importation of Vaisnavism that Nepalis were exposed to this particular concept. But Vaisnavism was a religion of an elite group. Under the Guptas a small number of Brahmins appeared and were appointed as temple priests, while the kings took the title of Kshatriyas. The people remained mainly Shiva-worshipping and non-caste, as shown by the large number of inscriptions from the period (Vajracharya, 1973). The Licchavi kings, as opposed to the Guptas, were also often Shiva worshippers. For example, the famous king Amsuvarma took the title 'Pashupati Bhattaraka' for himself, Pashupati being the primary Nepali form of Shiva. There appears to have been no attempt made to include the majority of the people within the caste system, so that only references to Brahmins and Kshatriyas have been found and the caste system remained a localized, isolated, and exotic plaything of the elite group.

After the Shaivites, the second largest religious group during ancient times was Buddhist. Even the Licchavi rulers themselves were very much influenced by Mahayana Buddhism, prevalent in north India at that time, and in the indigenous development of the Vajrayana forms of Buddhism. Vajrayana Buddhism was later adopted by Tibet where it was to flourish.

There are quite a few magnificent examples of Licchavi architecture in Patan, including the recently rebuilt Buddhist Mahavihara (monastery) on top of Danagiri hill at Pulchok. This is believed to have been built during the reign of King Amsuvarma, sometime in the seventh century (*Rising Nepal*, Feb. 27, 1986). The presence of shrines to Acheswor Mahadeva (Shiva, the great god) and Chandeshwari Bhagavati (a Tantric deity) within the monastery grounds typifies the religious syncretism found in Nepal. However, this religious flexibility began to change with the arrival of an increasing number of high caste Hindus, especially those with a markedly hostile attitude towards Buddhism. Having been threatened with extermination by the ruthless and aggressive Islamic Jehad, which was systematically erasing all traces of Hinduism in northern India, those Hindus who came into the Kathmandu Valley and western hills remained agitated and active in the preservation of their religion and lifestyle. The visit of Sankaracharya from south India at the end of the first millenium was particularly devastating for Buddhism and its followers and disruptive to the traditional worship of Shiva. Shiva, in the indigenous form of Pashupatinath, originally spoke through shamans, acting through their trances, appearing in their dreams, and was worshipped in cephalic linga forms. Yet at the end of the Licchavi period, Sankaracharya was able to convince the Nepali king, Shiva Deva, to have Brahmins appointed with exclusive privileges to act as priests at the Pashupatinath temple in Kathmandu. The fact that the major temples had to be staffed by Brahmin priests gave them high ritual status at the political level, and they were endowed with land grants which gave them economic independence.

The changes that took place at this time were aggressively implemented. Non-Brahmanic literature was destroyed in public book burning and much of the cultural heritage of the Licchavi period was lost in this process. Very little remains today apart from its architectural remnants. Many older social institutions were possibly eliminated at this time. Such a challenge to the essentially Buddhist hegemony could only have succeeded if supported by a powerful faction, which was most probably Shaivitic, with deep resentment of the then current regime. Buddhism was a religion of the plains, associated with particular dynastic groups whose avowed heritage was Indian. It was always essentially alien to Nepalis, who remained, intrinsically, Shamanistic-Shaivites. Sanka racharya's missionary fanaticism only succeeded to the extent that it was complemented with a nationalistic or ethnic based determination to revitalize a more ancient and indigenous society, freed from these foreign trappings. Candidates for these powerful allies are Kirati aristocrats, descended from earlier rulers, who regarded the 'Indian' families as intruders and their Buddhist-Vaisnavic culture as foreign. The Sankaracharya-initiated revolution succeeded in eventually toppling Licchavi society, but in the ensuing turmoil an even more alien social regime was imposed. By the beginning of the next millenium, Buddhist institutions were noticeably overshadowed by those of the high caste Hindus and their public rituals, and the Buddhist viharas (monasteries) were in the decline. Nepal was increasingly gravitating towards the influence of the caste structure. Buddhism, 'a religion which has been acclaimed as the highest expression of Asiatic humanism, which spread throughout the countries of the Middle and Far East, refining customs, art and literature, wiping out misunderstanding and prejudice, shattering the bond of caste and promising peace and redemption for all; the religion which led primitive Nepali society to the dawn of civilization', lost out completely in the land of its birth (Gnoli, 1984: 19). No more Buddhist structures were added, though many temples for the different Hindu deities were being built.

*Descriptions of Licchavi Culture*

The marriage of Princess Bhrikuti to King Tsrong Tsen Gampo of Tibet and the reception of Wang Hiuen Tse at the court of Narendra Dev (643-690 A.D.) are occasions which brought Nepali civilization into the wider world perspective. The account of the Licchavi court made by the Chinese ambassador, Wang Hiuen Tse, as quoted by Sylvain Levi (1905-8), describes splendours of the Licchavi period:

> The kingdom of Ni-po-lo is due west of Tou-fan (Tibet). Their king Na-ling-ti-po (Narendra Deva) wears pearls, rock crystals, mother of pearl, corals and amber, he has golden earrings and jade pendants, trinkets on his waist-belt adorned with a Foutou (Buddha). They sit on a seat supported by lions, in the interior of the hall where flowers and perfume are scattered. The eminent people, the officers and the whole court, are sitting to the right and to the left on the ground; beyond them are drawn up hundreds of armed soldiers.
>
> In the centre of the palace there is a tower of seven storeys, covered with copper tiles. Balustrades, railings, columns, and beams are all encrusted with stones and jewels. At each of the four corners of the tower water is poured into the troughs; from the dragon's mouth it gushes out as it would from a fountain.
>
> The father of Na-ling-ti-po was dethroned by his younger brother; Na-ling-ti-po had to flee to escape from his uncle. Tou-fan gave him refuge and re-established him on the throne; he consequently became their vassal.

He continues:

> The merchants, whether itinerant dealers or established ones, are numerous. They have copper coins which bear on one side a man's face and on the reverse a horse. The cultivators are few and they do not know how to plough the earth with the bulls. They do not perforate the nostrils of their bulls. The inhabitants are accustomed to shave their hair to the very edge of their eyebrows. They pierce their ears and introduce into the perforations little bamboo tubes. They eat with their hands without using

> spoons or sticks. All their utensils are made of copper. They dress themselves with one piece of cloth which covers the body. They bathe several times daily. Their houses are built of wood; the walls are sculptured and painted. They are very fond of scenic spots, are pleased to blow the horn and to beat the drum. They are fairly conversant with the reckoning of fate and in the researches of physical philosophy. They are equally smart in the art of the calendar. They venerate five celestial beings and carve their images on stone; each day they wash themselves with purifying water. They cook a sheep and offer it as a sacrifice.

The Licchavis helped to develop Nepal by promoting urban culture, a fine degree of craftsmanship, trade with Tibet, and a philosophy of syncretism in religion by introducing Vaisnavism and by observing all three religions, Shaivism, Mahayana Buddhism, and Vaisnavism with equal respect. The earliest and one of the finest urban centres in Nepal was established at Patan by Bir Dev in 299 A.D., while Kathmandu became a prominent urban site under Gunakama Deva in 732 A.D.. The population is thought to have been less than 30,000 in Patan, while that at Kathmandu was close to 50,000 during the Licchavi period. All of this had been possible with the flourishing profitable trade and commerce with both the Tibetans and the Indians (Dhungel, 1987: 168-73).

### THE MEDIEVAL PERIOD

It was only at the end of the first millenium that the fragmentation of the early Licchavi empire into a number of small states began and there arose two other powerful kingdoms, both of which began to threaten the Kingdom of Nepal with its capital in Kathmandu. One was the Kingdom of the Magars, with their centre in Palpa, west of Kathmandu, and the other was the Kingdom of the Khas in the far western region, with twin capitals at Dullu and Sinja. The rulers of all three came under the influence of the caste system then prevalent in India, which, in its adapted Nepali form, will be here referred to as Bahunism. By the fourteenth century, the Mallas had assumed dominance of the Kathmandu Valley; a dominance that was to last till the eighteenth century. Something of a cultural renewal began with the advent of Malla rule. Under the Mallas, Hinduism with a stratified caste system and fatalistic hierarchy was actively supported and Buddhism, with its strong connection with Tibet, was actively discouraged. The systematic maltreatment of the Buddhists and Buddhist monastic institutions continued. King Jayasthitiraja Malla (1295-1382), advised by the Maithili Brahmins from Bihar, enforced a caste order with a scheme of sixty-four occupational sub-castes within it. The caste hierarchy had become attractive because it helped enforce a social stability which could ensure the preservation of the Malla kingdom, which had not yet been fully secured and legitimated. The Kathmandu Valley was effectively closed as its society ceased to accept later arrivals into its urban fold and by the end of the fourteenth century Nepali society had become quite rigid. On the positive side, throughout the fifteenth and sixteenth century the Mallas developed Nepali literature, fine arts,metal casting,wood carving and architecture, while there was general economic prosperity based on trade.

Fatalistic hierarchy became more entrenched in Kathmandu society as the Malla dominance continued. In 1650, King Siddhinarsingh Malla decreed that anyone who had travelled to Tibet, the remaining stronghold of Buddhism, had to be purified on his return. This step stimulated a process of alienation from Tibet which had contributed so much to Nepali prosperity by way of trade in the past. Merchants engaging in Tibetan trade were subjected to humiliating rites as they were regarded as impure by the Hindu high caste people. Siddhinarsingh's Hinduism and fatalistic faith was so fervent that he eventually abdicated his throne and disappeared to become a Sannyasi[2].

The other areas which attracted hierarchic caste culture during the medieval period outside the Nepal valley were the flourishing Khas empire, centred in the Karnali river basin, and the powerful Magar kingdom, with its capital at Palpa. Once adopted by the Khas and Magars, the hierarchic caste culture and fatalistic faiths moved along the hills eastward with these people. The Khas had been successful in creating their own empire, including parts of Kashmir, western Tibet (Ngari province), and Kaligandaki, from the eleventh century to the sixteenth century (Tucci, 1956). The Khas state did not develop a flourishing urban centre of art and luxury as the Newars had done. They maintained their martial prowess with a simple lifestyle, largely determined by the ecology of the area they occupied.

The empire initially patronized Buddhism. With the introduction of hierarchic caste system and fatalistic faith, Khas society, too, began to ossify and by the sixteenth century the western Khas empire disintegrated. The Khas areas initially disintegrated into twenty-two kingdoms (Baisi rajya). Meanwhile the neighbouring Gandaki area, previously under Licchavi and partially under Magar rule, developed into twenty-four kingdoms (Chaubishi rajya). During the fifteenth century Kathmandu Valley itself was divided by the three sons of King Yakshya Malla (1428-82) into three kingdoms and the name Nepal was monopolized by the kingdom of Kathmandu alone. It was only during the eighteenth century that the Khas, Bahun, Gurung, and Magar provided the military might under the leadership of King Prithvi Narayan Shah of the kingdom of Gorkha, one of the twenty-four rajyas of the Gandaki area, to unite the disintegrated states into a form which could hold its own throughout the colonial period[3]. A primary difference between Gorkha and the other kingdoms of Nepal was that it had not been hierarchized as much by the caste system as the areas west of it and the Kathmandu Valley, and hence had not been dissipated by fatalism and its negative influence. Instead of being a rigid, fatalistic society, Gorkhas still lived by ancient principles which allowed a large measure of egalitarianism and personal initiative for achievement.

In 1816, the Sugauli Treaty was signed with the British East India Company, which defined the boundaries of present day Nepal. The Khas language, which had become the lingua franca in wide areas for quite some time by then, became the official Nepali national language, though the Newari language remains paramount within the Kathmandu Valley. In 1847, a Khas general secured a position of power soon after he became the Prime Minister and took the title of Rana for himself and his family imitating the Indian Rajput style, and his family later became the hereditary Prime Ministers and effectively ruled the country until 1950.

*The Ranas*

During the nineteenth century British influence from the Indian plains grew and many Nepalis were enticed to serve in British military regiments. The Rana regime actively supported and encouraged the export of the able-bodied manpower to British India. The relationship between certain groups of Nepalis and the British grew to be a strong one, a consequence of which was that the loyalty and attachment of hundreds of thousands of Nepalis was directed away from their own land towards a foreign power. National pride and sentiment were very much diluted and essentially centred around very narrow and limited areas of their locale and their own kin groups. Little effort was made to promote patriotism and loyalty towards the state of Nepal. In fact, an enlightened patriotism was punished by the ruling Ranas as they felt threatened by it. As the Ranas were holding absolute power over the country and exploiting the resources mainly for their own benefit, the people they could trust were those who were exclusively loyal to them alone. Anyone with a concern for the society at large and to the future of the country had to be the enemy of the Ranas. So they singled out, punished, jailed and executed anyone who fought for the people's welfare on the pretext that it was high treason. Many Nepalis in outlying areas did not even bother to question this state of affairs. The bulk of the able-bodied members of the population were quite familiar with the name of the British monarch and conditions in India because of the connections to those who were serving the British Empire, while the powerful Ranas chose to surround themselves with dependent sycophants and opportunists, contributing to the degeneration of ethical and moral principles of the people around the seat of power.

## RECENT EMERGENCE FROM FEUDAL PERIOD

At the end of World War II a large number of countries won independence from their colonial overlords. The first task of these nations was to develop an integrated national state loyal to their own traditional, native power-base or to a democratically elected native government, composed of people from among themselves. This has not been an easy task anywhere among the large number of countries which are collectively called the 'Third World'. With few exceptions, many Third World countries are still struggling for economic self-sufficiency and political stability. Though colonialism has its dark side, in many cases colonial administrations left behind certain positive legacies that were advantageous to modernization. Colonial administrations developed transportation systems, established a basic educational system and introduced a modern system of administration. Nepal has no colonial background, and by comparison to those that have, the country has suffered from the absence of a developmental infrastructure of any kind whether institutional or in terms of physical facilities. In some cases, this isolation and lack of colonial experience was an advantage, but otherwise this left the country in a far worse condition compared to other Third World countries under colonial rule. Nepal was kept under the worst form of isolation, backwardness and economic exploitation and the country remained a feudal estate controlled by the Ranas. Their only interest was the collection of revenue and maintenance of law and order. It was only in 1950, in the wake of its liberation from Rana family rule, that the country emerged from a very medieval form of feudal dominance.

NOTES AND REFERENCES

1. The caste or varna system was based on five primary social classifications: the Brahmin (priest), the Kshatriya(warrior or administrator), the Vaisya (merchant), the Shudra (labourer), and the untouchable (or polluted).
2. It was only discovered recently that he died at the age of seventy-one as a Sannyasi Sadhu in Benares (personal communication from Dhanavajra Vajracharya).
3. From this period the Khas, Magar and Gurung began to be known collectively to outsiders by the name of Gurkha or Gorkhali.

CHAPTER TWO

# THE CASTE SYSTEM IN NEPAL

Though Nepal is considered to have long been Hindu, its native Hinduism has not included a belief in caste principles, which remain a foreign importation with little popular support. Only in the past hundred and thirty-five years has the caste system gained any kind of endorsement[1] . Though supported only by a minority of the populace, it is a very important minority, socially located to mediate the relations between Nepal and the outside world. Nepal's access to the outside world and its reaction to external influence are determined by the members of this group. Their personal response limits the response of the entire nation. If, as a group, they are astute, ambitious, and high achievers, with a sense of commitment, national pride and self-confidence, a rapid and efficient Nepali adaptation to social and technological change can be expected. But as a group these critically positioned people do not have these qualities; instead they are the victims of their own fatalistic beliefs, poor self image, hierarchic caste status and constant defensiveness; and the cumulative effect of these characteristics is to hamper national development through inactivity and conservative reaction (Khanal, 1987). In this chapter we will see just how isolated this section of the population is in their attitudes, outlook, and what the social context of their position is really like.

Within Nepal, religion is a very important aspect of human life. The Nepali word for religion is *dharma*, which also means duty, ethics, morality, rule, merit and pious acts. Therefore, when Nepalis discuss religion they understand it with a broader meaning than is usually applied in the West. Hinduism is the official religion of Nepal. The label Hinduism is applied broadly to many religious systems practised. in southern Asia, east of the Indus. In Nepal Hinduism includes Shamanism, and hence religions derived from the early Gopal and Kirat traditions, as well as Brahmanism[2], the version of Hinduism brought from India. When the Nepali Bureau of Statistics states that ninety per cent of the population are Hindus, people do not understand this to mean that the bulk of the population are orthodox Hindus. Nepalis have never been orthodox nor are they ever likely to be. The state automatically assumes that everyone is Hindu unless they specifically declare themselves otherwise.

Buddhism has always been the second religion, though it must be understood that Hinduism in its liberal form incorporates Buddhism as a sect or branch within it. In the high Himalayan settlements, people of Tibetan background practise a form of Mahayana Buddhism popularly called Lamaism. The second largest group practising the Mahayana (or Vajrayana) form of Buddhism is that of a section of the Newars of the Kathmandu Valley, where it has been practised from the earliest times to the present day.

The present constitution declares that the king has to be a Hindu but it does not prohibit Nepalis from practising other religions. Nevertheless, state law prohibits any kind of formal proselytization or conversion from one religion to another. Such prohibition is the result of the perception of a connection between missionary activity and colonialism.

While there has been a general synthesizing tendency, the history of religion in Nepal has not always been a peaceful one, even though it is frequently described that way. Ancient and early medieval history has been documented by high-caste Brahmanic scholars whose interests have not facilitated the most comprehensive and objective depiction of Nepali history. Their documentation is limited by a Gangetic Hindu world view. This world view is insensitive to historical factors outside the general ambit of the Puranic tradition and overlooks both the late arrival of the fatalistic caste system and its relatively tenuous position within Nepali culture. It also overlooks the fact that the various ethnic communities within Nepal were undergoing a significant process of change throughout the Licchavi period, and that this was not happening because of their exposure to the Hindu culture of the Gangetic basin alone. In fact, they had an equally strong cultural and economic relationship with Tibet.

References to conflict between Gangetic Hinduism and the other religious traditions observed within Nepal have been obscured. The instances of the Pashupat-Shaivite Kirat being driven away by the Licchavis, the suppression of the Buddhists by the Shaivite and Vaishnavic Hindus, the rebellious struggle of Ghantakarna against the stratified caste system, are some of the instances which have not been as well documented. The imposition of a southern Shaiva priesthood within the Pashupatinath temple precincts, and the refusal of later Licchavi kings to worship Vishnu (though they had been proclaimed to personally embody Vishnu), also imply much religious and social turmoil (Acharya, 1970: 24). There is a declaration by Amsu Varma in *Bugmati*, dated 604 A.D, which stated that disputes between different religious groups were to be adjudicated by the royal court itself (Vajracharya, 1973), which suggests both that such religious conflicts did exist and were serious enough to require the king's personal attention.

Many recent anecdotes illustrating the initial resistance to foreign religious systems and ideas can be found from the Khas area of the Karnali river basin. For example, a descendant of the first immigrant Bahun(Brahman) into the lower basin of the Humla Karnali related an incident concerning his ancestor's encounter with the local Shamans of the Gura Mashta[3], a powerful local divinity. The Bahun informant recounted that:

> . . . after having an argument with his ancestor Gura Mashta was very annoyed and concerned about being defeated or overshadowed by the Bahun. So Gura Mashta cursed him by saying that he (the newly arrived opponent) and his male descendants would never have the qualities of being both handsome and having beautiful voices at the same time. If one had a handsome body and complexion, he would have a bad voice; if he happened to have a beautiful voice, he would be physically ugly. With this compromise the Bahun immigrant was allowed not only to reside in the region but also to have clients following his ritual leadership. (Personally communicated to this author by Karna Prashad Bhatta,the former member of the National Panchayat from Humla).

In some ways both the new version of Hindu religion introduced by the recently arriving Bahuns and the existing Shamanistic faith cooperated, as each was convinced that the other was being subsumed into its own prevalent faith. Neither hierarchic Hinduism nor Shamanistic religions required any formal process of conversion, and neither had any problem with variations in the form of ritual practice. Hindu Bahuns believed that once people developed faith in the divine origin of castes everything would fall into place automatically. Nor did the practice of spirit worship and spirit possession by Shamans contradict the popular form of Hindu religion. The practice of appeasing spiritual forces by blood sacrifice was ultimately compatible with both systems. Bahun priests were not opposed as long as they were able to make a living by having a few clients who commissioned them for certain rituals and paid their *dakshina* (fees). Similarly, the Shamans did not mind because the new Hindu priests did not wean their clients away from them altogether, agreed to accept the higher position of the Shamans and maintained their ritual distance from the Shamans (Berreman, 1964).

Ancestor worship was part of the ritual which the Brahmanic Hindu religion did not object to being maintained. The difference in the rituals of these two religions was hardly noticeable. The new priests invoked the spirit through Vedic incantations while the Shamans' medium was an old language which was equally incomprehensible and esoteric as far as the common people were concerned. So there is no difference between a Bahun or a Dhami-Shaman officiating. It further appears that many ambitious Khas Dhamis (Shamans) adopted Bahun caste status and continued their priestly role. Anthropologists who have studied the belief system of the people in that area have pointed out the caste and the ethnic background of the Dhamis of the area. There are a number of Bahun, Thakuri, Chhetri, Khas and untouchables who have taken the role of Dhami (Gaborieau, 1976).

Generally, the people tolerated the incoming new system as long as it did not try to contradict their own religious faith and practice. The local chiefs and upper classes had no problem in adopting the social forms of this religion as it gave them a hierarchic structure wherein they could attain high positions of power and authority for themselves without having to give up any of the privileges which they already enjoyed. This was the beginning of the process of stratification of the Khas society and the infusion of the fatalistic faith into it. The Hindu Puranas have been fashionable teachings, adding prestige and status as well as a sense of modernity, coming as they did from a society in the Gangetic plains which had always been more prosperous, prestigious and powerful than Nepal. But people outside these privileged classes were not willing to accept a religion which imposed upon them a very low status within the social and ritual hierarchy. As far as the adoption of new divinities into the spiritual pantheon was concerned, there was no particular problem because they continued to worship the original ones along with the new. Prayag R. Sharma, who studied the society and its activities, made a perceptive observation that even the multitude of gods worshipped by the Khas who have adopted widespread Brahmanical values have peculiar sounding names quite unfamiliar to the Brahmanical pantheon (Sharma, 1971:45-6)[4]. In the course of time many people throughout the country adopted Vishnu and other deities in addition to the primordial god Shiva or Pashupatinath and came to be known as Hindus.

Generally speaking the religious syncretism attributed to Nepali society is mostly confined to the Kathmandu Valley, and particularly to the Newars. Elsewhere, other ethnic groups are more singular in their worship, which tends to be predominantly Shamanistic with few inroads by these other belief systems. As already indicated, the Tibetan-speaking peoples of the high Himalayas are an exception as they have integrated Buddhism with their Shamanic practices (Holmberg, 1989). While the people of the Kathmandu Valley were happy to add the entertainment value of new and exotic rituals into their festival repertoire, they were resistant to the elimination of their native beliefs, and preferred to integrate a plurality of belief and ritual systems rather than submit to the subjugation or overthrow of their treasured traditions. This was true of their integration of Shamanism and Shaivism, as well as with Vaishnavism and Buddhism. Such an integration has been facilitated by the fact that the Newars have never been particularly interested in issues of ideology. Colin Rosser, after a careful study of Newar society, observed that:

> '...it is incredibly difficult, if not impossible, to identify the vast bulk of the Newar population as being either Hindu or Buddhist. The degree of religious syncretism is so complex that such a distinction on grounds of belief and ritual practice is out of the question... and it is important to note that this distinction is not generally made by the Newars themselves... [There are] many cases throughout the Kathmandu Valley of individual Newar families employing a Brahman for some of its domestic rituals and a Gubhaju [Buddhist priest] for others within the same household, and that sometimes, indeed, both priests would be present at the same time. (Rosser, 1966: 79).

Often religious practices are synthesized. There is a practice of worshipping Pashupatinath as Buddha, for example, on a Full Moon Day of November every year. Similarly, recognizing him as an incarnation of a Bhairav, Shiva is offered blood sacrifice and frequently offered buffalo meat on a number of occasions.Many people, particularly the Tamang Lamas, consider Avalokiteswora (Chen re si) to be an incarnation of Shiva (Holmberg, 1989). The Tantric rituals were mixed with Vaisnava; Vaisnava with Shaiva, and Shaiva with Buddhist Vajrayana. For example, there is a Krishna statue in the Buddhist temple compound of Kwa Baha in Patan, and there are statues of Vishnu, Rama and Buddha in Pashupatinath. Many deities in a number of temples in the Kathmandu Valley are worshipped as different deities of various cults with separate backgrounds outside Nepal. Matsendranath is worshipped by Shaiva, Buddhist, and tantric Nepalis with equal zeal and devotion. Worship of the Hindu chthonic deities has been integrated with the Shamanistic pantheon, so that Bhumi Devta or the Shipta Than, Udhauli-Ubhauli, Bhut, Pret, Vayu, Naga, the indigenous deities, and supernatural spirits who took care of the worldly needs of the local people now form an integrated cluster. Mashta, originally the god of the Khas in the west, is also believed by the Bahun priests of the area to be the son of Indra, the Vedic god. Since this god speaks directly and acts in person through the oracle, the Dhami, this oracle is considered to be more powerful than the Bahun priests in this region. For example, an illiterate Dhami, oracle of Tharpa, another powerful Mashta of the region, is believed to have the knowledge of all the Vedic texts through his god. Local Bahun priests, not being properly educated themselves abide by this, and stand corrected on occasions when the Dhami interrupts their recitation of Vedic hymns.

## HISTORY OF THE CASTE SYSTEM

Though Nepal has long been Hindu in a very general sense, a stratified caste system has only marginally penetrated its society which is confined to particular classes of particular ethnic groups. Nepal's early connection with Hinduism was through the worship of Pashupatinath who was identified with Shiva. The form of Shaivism that developed in Nepal was always close to its Shamanistic and animistic roots. It had little to do with the Puranas and it had no connections with any form of caste system. Caste concepts only entered Nepal for the first time in the beginning of the Licchavi era, in the form of Vaishnavism, and when it did arrive it had to adapt itself not only to Shamanism and Shaivism but also to Buddhism.

The Licchavis and, in particular, the Guptas styled themselves Kshatriyas (Chhetri) and maintained Brahmans (Bahuns) from the south as their personal priests. The oldest inscription that categorically mentions Bahun inhabitants was found in Thankot, consecrated by King Vasant Deva in the fifth century (Vajracharya, 1973: 91-93). But the Gupta kings do not appear to have imposed a division of labour and craft specialization on the basis of a caste system (Panta, *Purnima*, I. 2: 1-10). Though elements of caste were introduced (as evident in the designations of Bahun and Chhetri), the caste system in its entirety was never adopted; during this period the actual social organization of Kathmandu Valley society continued as before, with its pre-existing class structures. The discrepancy between the popular religion and that of the elites was reinforced by the priestly Brahman's lack of interest in creating a local priesthood. Instead, they were interested only in creating client castes.

The Bahun caste was to consist only of Indian Brahman migrants, and while they may have maintained their own levels of ritual purity it is not at all clear whether their new Nepali clients similarly laboured to maintain caste purity.

While Chhetri designations are used there is no documentary evidence that Kshatriya rituals were observed. The priests were willing to initiate the upper class Khas, Magar and Newar as Chhetri, but the Chhetri status was expensive to maintain and the priests constantly demanded a high fee from them, such as endowment of tax-free lands in exchange for officiating at rituals. Consequently only a small number of Khas and Magar took the Chhetri title, mainly with an interest to legitimize their upper class position within the society. Those that would have qualified as Vaishya or Shudra saw no advantage in becoming part of the caste system and none among the shoemakers, blacksmiths, goldsmiths, tanners or tailors were willing to accept the position of the untouchables. Even today among the people of Kathmandu Valley, most of these occupational classes are not treated as untouchables. The Nepali people appear to have preferred an open social order rather than one based on caste principles as is prevalent in India, where there is much emphasis on the dialectics of the pure and the impure (Dumont, 1970).

Any attempt to impose a caste system on a society must be an ambitious one, as the bulk of the population must be in a position where it cannot resist the humiliating circumstances that the caste designations represent. Caste essentially involves the ascription of qualities of graduated social pollution, with the most polluted becoming pariahs. No one will volunteer to become a low caste. Merchants also have to be willing to assume a measure of pollution and a low status, which is problematic for a society whose affluence is based on trade, as was the case with fourteenth century Kathmandu[5]. Nepal may have had sharp class inequalities, but it has never had endemic class oppression, which is necessary for a caste system to be firmly introduced. Nepali culture contains too much egalitarianism to favour the development of a genuine caste system. But the attempt has been made and it is having negative consequences, especially since the middle of the nineteenth century.

Historically, it appears that the caste system has its greatest success when called upon to help establish the legitimacy of a particular regime. With the destruction or elimination of Buddhist institutes of scholarship at the end of the first millenium, the Bahun pundits have become the sole vehicle of erudition. They are the writers, the repository and the interpreters of history, and for appropriate consideration have been quick to document the ancient illustrious status of any new reign. The last historic incident was when they had Jung Bahadur Kunwar, a Khas, adopt the title of Rana, developing a fictitious ancestry of Rajput origin from the southern plains. Certain similarities in language and cultural traits exist between the Khas people and those of Rajasthan and Gujarat, all of whom are believed to have migrated across the Karakoram during the prehistoric period and to have spread over the western Himalayas as well as the Punjab, Rajastan and Gujarat (Sharma, Janak Lal, 1982: 243). This made it easier for the advisers of Jung Bahadur to posit a connection with the Rajputs of the plains, even though any study of the ancestors of Jung Bahadur Rana leads to the conclusion that the Ranas were Khas, who took the title of Kunwar (prince) during the medieval period but had no connection with the Indian Rajputs (Whelpton, 1987).

A sense of insecurity among certain Pundits have led them to concoct fictitious genealogies for any ruling dynasty they want, who then have been deemed to be of Indian origin. If this were true, it would seem that the Nepali people are, as a whole, incapable of ruling themselves. There has never been a conquest of Nepal initiated from within India, so from the interpretation of history we are forced to infer that these so-called Indian dynasties must have secured their position through invitation, as a result of their personal superiority over anything that Nepalis had to offer. It is very hard to believe that Nepalis, with their reputation for an independent spirit and martial qualities, could not produce their own leaders but had to wait for fugitive nobles to arrive from India and paid homage to them as soon as they set foot in the hills. There is evidence suggesting that such Indian pedigrees for the Thakuri-Chhetri are the artifacts of their own sycophants.

In all my research I have been unable to discover any genuine evidence that any Thakuri (aristocratic) family has its origins in India. Instead there is some evidence of distinctly Nepali origins for most Thakuris and Chhetris. For example, Nepali people have clan and family tutelary deities with clearly indigenous origins, and these deities have their own ritual practices and even their own local (typically Shamanistic) priesthood. An Indian family is extremely unlikely to have created for itself such a non-Brahmanic tutelary deity and is further unlikely to have it attended by non-Brahmans: so that the presence of such a deity, with non-Bahun priests, may be taken as indicating an indigenous origin. The Shah Thakuris have been given a Rajput ancestry by a few historians, yet all their clan deities and family tutelary deities are worshipped and cared for exclusively by Magars — by Brahmanic standards a polluted low caste ethnic group; the Gorkha Kali, Manakamana, and the goddess at Lasargha, are in the exclusive care of the Magars[6]. This trend has been the major means by which the Bahun pundits have attempted to gain influence and expand the hierarchic caste system. The main consequence has been a major distortion of Nepali history, belittling Nepali achievement while reorienting the culture evermore towards that of the Gangetic plains.

After the Bahun and Thakuri, the next highest caste group is that of the Chhetri. Various people of high status from among those groups that played an active part in the unification of Nepal took the title of Chhetri shortly afterwards. But not all Chhetris come from this background, and the proportion that do is ever decreasing, particularly within the Kathmandu Valley. Those others that have the title of Chhetri are the children of Bahun fathers and indigenous ethnic mothers. As Bahuns move into new areas, these mixed Chhetri children form the nucleus of the caste community. Such children differ from the local Matwali children in being given an education by their fathers, and often tend to be successful economically and socially. These Chhetri then become the clients of the Bahun priests, with their economic success providing the basis of their economic support. Their educational and economic distinctiveness facilitates their elevation to high status within the local community, which then influences the infusion of fatalism and hierarchic caste principles into local ethnic life.

A majority of the Bahun priests are the descendants of caste Brahmans who came mainly from the plains, though with some smaller groups from the Deccan during the medieval period. A few may have come to the Nepal region for purposes of proselytizing but most were forced to emigrate from hostile invasions of the plain states. In particular, there were to be many who were running away from the religious persecutions of the Moslems. These people did not bring any religious mission with them but an excessive concern for self-preservation which was to affect their relations profoundly with the inhabitants of Nepal and Nepali culture. The preservation of caste culture required that they did not succumb to Nepali influence nor in any way diminish the purity of their cultural treasures. The defence of their culture lead readily to the depreciation of the cultural lifestyle of the Nepalis. Benares and other sacred cities of India represented, for them, the ideals of urban civilization, and Kathmandu's culture was denigrated.The river water in Benares continues to be treated as holier than the clean and fresh water of all the Himalayan rivers of Nepal. As the Muslim occupation of the south continued there was a general lapse in orthodoxy. What persevered was a continuing denigration of Nepali culture and Nepali people in general and an exaggerated adulation of the fatalistic caste culture of the plains with their religious centres such as Benares being treated as the holiest places of pilgrimage. This denigration of Nepali culture has become an inherent aspect of the developed Nepali form of Hinduism with a fatalistic hierarchy as interpreted by Bahun priests.

Hindu caste culture has a varied presence in Nepal, in terms of its prevalence and its significance. In the next sections of this chapter I will consider its distribution in the major regions of Nepal, starting with the area where it has the strongest presence, the Kathmandu Valley.

### *The Kathmandu Valley*

During the latter part of the fourteenth century, King Jayasthitiraj Malla tried to purify religious practice in the Kathmandu Valley by introducing caste principles and conduct according to the Manusmriti code of the Hindus (Lamsal, 1966: 38). He did this as a measure towards modernization, little realizing that it would lead the society to regression rather than progression. He developed many rules for the wearing of certain types of clothing and ornamentation and for the construction of houses, differentiated according to caste levels, and made it punishable for anyone to violate rules prescribing professional activities for different castes. Such efforts were not successful. The people continued their old habits of eating buffalo meat and drinking alcohol, as required by their traditional festivals and worship practices. According to the *Vamsavali* chronicle, a Shiva Datta Maithili Brahman, who had come from India, objected that the sacred thread-wearing people, called generally Tagadhari, were eating buffalo meat. This led the king to ask the Nepalis to choose between eating buffalo meat and giving up the sacred thread. The people argued that they had to offer buffalo meat and alcohol to their patron deity, Taleju Bhavani, and consequently gave up wearing the sacred thread (ibid., 31). The priestly Bahuns, in spite of their efforts to gain political support for their superior role, remained basically outside the mainstream of Nepali culture and civilization of the time, but their attempts to introduce the caste system persisted. Kathmandu valley society having already developed to a high level of urban civilization and culture, the Bahun priests could hardly contribute anything for further improvement except help legitimatize the Malla rule by concocting a theory to prove their Rajput background[7].

The Kathmandu Valley was effectively closed towards the latter part of the Malla period. The people of Nepal valley came to be known as the 'Newar' during the fifteenth century, in the reign of Pratap Malla of Kathmandu (Acharya Baburam, 1972:6). These were the urban technical professionals, the majority of peasants and the working poor. Gradually this Newar society became a separate cultural group with its own rich urban-based culture. 'Kathmandu ceased to accept later arrivals into its urban fold, so the land gradually became known as 'Nepa[l]' and its people as 'Neva[r]' (Doherty, 1978; Malla, 1981). Then the two separated: the land retained its name, Nepal, but the people of the valley continued to be called Neva[r], which eventually gave rise to the process of search for an ancestry and origin separate from other Nepalis who did not speak the same language, Newari. During the eighteenth century, when the country expanded and several smaller states were reunited into Nepal, the Neva[r] people were treated as a separate ethnic group.

Another attempt at imposing the caste system was made in the nineteenth century by Jung Bahadur, a Khas, who was very keen to have his own status raised to the highest possible level. Jung Bahadur became the first of the Ranas and his task was to establish the legitimacy of the Ranas and secure Rana control over the land. He succeeded in introducing the caste system to a much greater degree than the Malla kings had done just over four hundred years before him. In the nineteenth century, the Khas Bahuns, now called Parvate *Bahun* (hill Bahun), decided to put all Newari-speaking people into a single caste category at the lower level, known in local parlance as Matwali, meaning *liquor drinkers* (see Figure 4). Even Bahuns who had been serving as Newari priests, the Newari Bahuns, lost ritual status vis-a-vis the 'pure Bahuns', the Parvate Bahuns, of the Khas language speaking community, which was dominant in the valley by that time. The old Newar upper caste, the Shrestha, were also reduced to Matwali status.

As a consequence, among Hindu Newars, caste has become more complex and stratified than among the non-Newar Bahun-Chhetri-Thakuri group. This latter group may consider all Newar people to be equally Matwali, and essentially of the Vaishya caste, but this is not the perception of the Newar themselves. Within the Matwali designation, then, can be found Newari Bahuns. These Bahuns have been much neglected by the unorthodox and somewhat egalitarian behaviour of Newar society, and are dwindling fast. Their number is very small and few are visible in any form of public life today. Then there are the Shresthas, including the old Newari aristocracy and upper class. Among the Shrestha there are two divisions—Cha-thare and Panch-thare. Chathare Shrestha are the Newari equivalent of Thakuri—the Malla, Pradhan, Amatya, etc. Panch-thare Shresthas are like the Chhetri among the Nepali-speaking people and have been drawn from multiple backgrounds, often from successful merchant families.

As a result of Jayasthitiraj Malla's attempt at classifying Kathmandu Valley society according to caste principles, Buddhist Newars have their own caste counterparts. Vajracharya are at the top like the Bahun; then there are the Sakya—sometimes calling themselves Sakyabhikshu. This indicates that they were ordained as Buddhist monks at some time in history.

The majority of the Kathmandu Valley people—peasants, farmers, vegetable growers, florists, potters, bricklayers and many other professions, are collectively called the Jyapu. Jyapu literally means 'competent worker' in the Newari language. Their significant contribution to Nepali society has never been formally recognized, so that the Jyapu have been a low status group, at least since medieval times. The Jyapu were turned into a low caste category during the Malla period, acquiring the designation of Shudra. Although some individual Jyapu families achieved Shrestha status through personal industry, mostly over several generations, they never managed this mobility as a group case similar to that of the Khas of the western hills. But the Jyapu remained united and never allowed themselves to be pushed into the position of serfdom or slavery as many non-Hindu indigenes in the plains were forced to do. They had a long history, were proud of their culture, had a strong internal social organization developed from ancient days, and were in control of the important means of production, namely the agricultural land. Jyapus are among the most progressive farmers in Nepal[8]. They are also the main group of people who take care of the communal festivals, religious dances, musical performances and important seasonal ceremonies in the Kathmandu Valley. In spite of their being labelled Shudra, Jyapus are still playing essential roles on many ritually important occasions, acting in roles which are usually filled only by high caste people. For example, Jyapus not only carry the statues of the deities and the ritual offerings but also cook food for them and for the high caste people of both Hindu and Buddhist backgrounds.

Many people speak of the caste system as if it were a representation of the classical Varna model, as prescribed in such ancient codes as the *Manusmriti* (diagram 1). But this original model has been greatly affected by many factors and does not exist in its original form anywhere in Nepal. It has been unorthodox and permeable from the beginning. The Bahun-Chhetri perspective on caste is represented in diagram 2. The Bahun are the Nepali Brahmans, the Chhetri, the Kshatriya, and the Matwali, the Vaishya and Shudra. The Thakuri and Shrestha are actually class labels that are also found outside of Bahunized societies. They are both aristocratic designa-

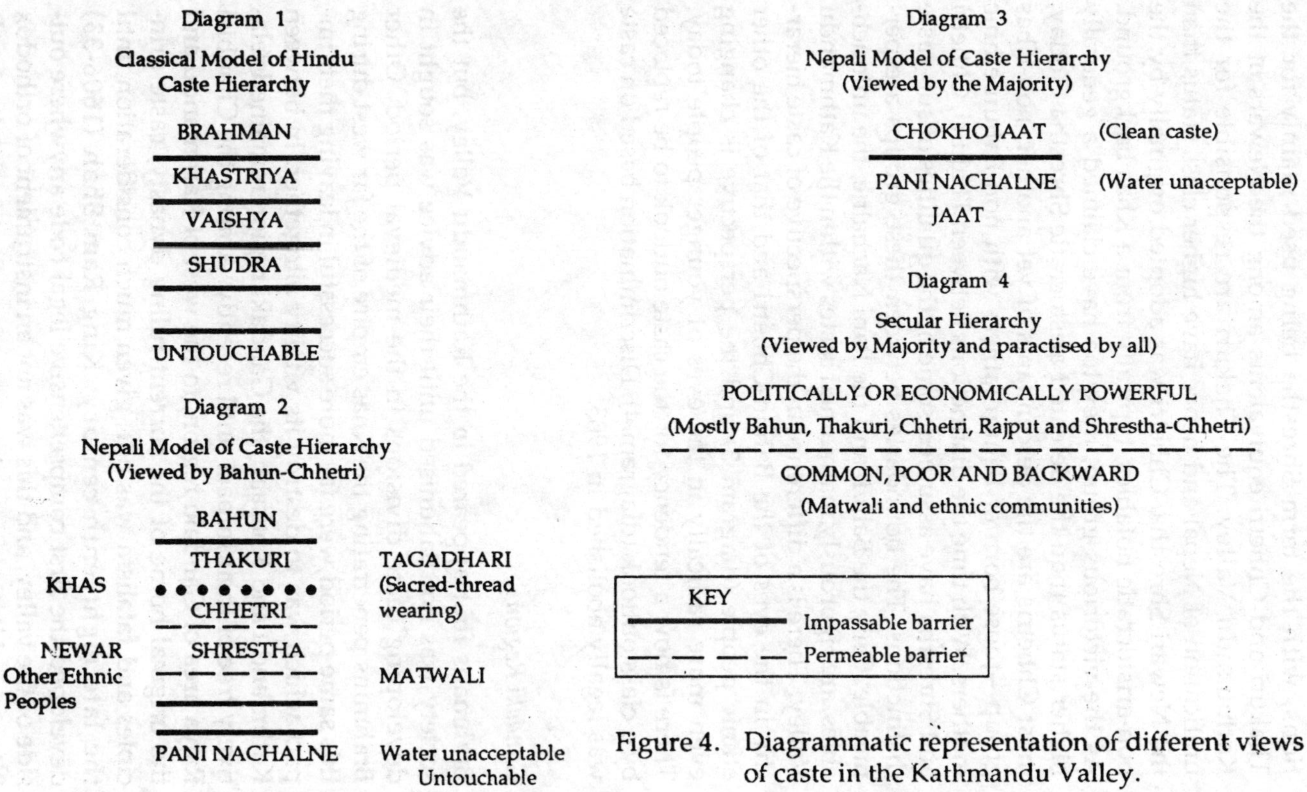


Figure 4. Diagrammatic representation of different views of caste in the Kathmandu Valley.

tions, with the term Shrestha being used mainly for the Thakuri and Chhetri equivalents among the Newars of the Kathmandu Valley. The Thakuri are responsible for the unification of Nepal and hence have higher class status than the Newari Shrestha. Chhetri was adopted originally by the non-aristocratic notables, typically from a Khas background. As the victorious group, they too have claimed a generally higher status than the defeated aristocratic Shrestha. Today, most Chhetris are the descendants of yet another, non-Khas group—those born of Bahun fathers with non-Bahun ethnic mothers. With time the distinctions between Thakuri, Chhetri and Shrestha have assumed some of the qualities of sub-caste distinctions. The boundaries between these groups are permeable. Only the Bahun and the Pani Nachalne, the untouchables, are rigorously maintained castes within the Kathmandu Valley. There is a difference in the perspective of caste hierarchy in the eyes of the Bahun-Chhetri and that of the other ethnic people (diagram 3) and the perspective is changing even more radically in the eyes of younger people today. There is now a tendency for the caste outlook to be replaced by a class outlook (diagram 4). Discrimination based on caste was legally abolished in 1963.

*Gandaki Region*

Brahmans first appeared in the Kathmandu Valley, but the society was not Bahunised until their advice was sought in developing caste divisions in the medieval period. Other Brahmins penetrating the Khas empire of the far west during this same period,were far more successful in leaving their impact which was to destroy its vitality altogether. In between Kathmandu and Khasaan, the Gandaki region remained relatively free of their impact until recently. Among the Chaubisi Rajya area of Gandaki region, to the west of Kathmandu and the original home of the current ruling dynasty, caste principles and fatalism was not given much consideration until the late eighteenth century. King Ram Shah (1606-33) developed the first comprehensive legal code anywhere outside of the valley, and this was not an instrument of orthodox hierarchic Hinduism, as has sometimes been mistakenly alleged by various scholars (see Joshi and Rose, 1966: 11-12).

On the contrary, his legal code became famous and was respected by all as a very fair and judicious system, a critical factor which facilitated the ready acceptance of the Gorkha rulers by all the people of Nepal.

King Prithvinarayan Shah, Ram Shah's descendant, continued this tradition and treated Bahuns as any other people, largely ignoring hierarchic caste prescriptions for the regulation of social behaviour. He considered the four castes and thirty-six ethnic groups, which he called 'chhattis varna', as equals. His campaign of unification had been successful in part because he had been able to recognize ethnic and regional pride and self-esteem among his followers. Rather than supporting orthodox caste practices, he encouraged Bahuns to be soldiers and professionals. He said that he had soldiers from four different peoples, namely, Bahun, Magar, Thakuri and Khas (Stiller, 1968), indicating that he saw Bahuns as being an ethnic social group without recognizing their association with caste. He certainly treated and employed Bahuns in a way different from their Bahunistic background, since they constituted part of his effective military force, which is unthinkable in any kind of orthodox situation. Among the documents of that time, there is no reference to the Chhetri, who were scarce in the Gandaki area until then. Bahun families from the areas around Gorkha i.e., Lamjung and Tanahu have been more enterprising, adaptive and progressive than their counterparts in the areas west of them. In the west they have been more successful in imposing Bahunistic values to the indigenous people and thus keep them fatalistically hierarchic and backward. Probably it was for this reason that Prithvi Narayan Shah advised his people not to trust the Khas-Bahun from the areas east and west.

The Bahuns of the Gandaki region, as with the Bahuns of the Kirat regions, migrated well after the time of their initially impelled movement into Nepal, consequent to the Islamic and other invasions of the Gangetic plains. They were less idealistic; forced to move primarily by economic circumstances rather than cultural or ideological infringement and oppression. With no caste panchayat to regulate behavior, the economic motivation in turn facilitated a drift towards unorthodoxy, as their traditional vocations, centered on the priesthood, failed to find viable support among the people and they were reduced to doing physical labour in order to survive.

With time, in some areas, being a Bahun simply meant being a member of just another ethnic group, and they worked in all occupations and even practised diverse religious beliefs with local origins. While there may have been Bahuns in these areas then, the presence of caste principles and the influence of fatalism was not directly proportionate to their numbers.

Generally it may be claimed that the absence of fatalism and stratified hierarchy in the Gandaki region facilitated Ghorka's successful reunification of the country. The people there, including many achievement oriented Bahun individuals, remained ambitious, with a strong sense of what they could personally achieve—a motivation crippled under the fatalistic tenets of the caste system. Ram Shah's code appealed to all Nepalis, who responded to its innate egalitarianism; a sense of justice for all, unlike the *Manusmriti* codes which promised legal discrimination and institutionalized social oppression. Such egalitarianism was consonant with their own sensibilities. Soon it became famous throughout the twenty- four kingdoms of the Gandaki region and people began to come to Gorkha for proper justice. The adage 'for knowledge go to Benares, and to Gorkha for justice' became widespread[9]. Kirkpatrick, a British East India Company official who visited Nepal in 1793 wrote of the Gorkhalis that:

> The superior class of these people admitted of considerable freedom in the carriage and the conversation of the lower orders, whom they were very rarely affected to keep at any distance. Nor was this sort of easy intercourse confined to particular description of men. It existed equally among the military and the civil ranks; the private soldier being as unembarassed and forward to deliver his sentiments in the presence of an officer of whatever degree, as the fisherman or porter before a minister of state, or governor. At the same time, this frankness of manner was never seen to degenerate into rudeness or disrespect (Kirkpatrick, 1964:36 reprint).

This clearly indicates the prevalence of native egalitarianism, and not the hierarchized social order of the hierarchic caste system. This came in much later to the Ghorkalis, specially after the introduction of the legal code of 1854.

*Khasaan*

Prithvinarayan Shah (1768-75) established his reign over a united Nepal in 1768 with the help of the Khas, Magar, Bahun, and Gurung peoples of the western hills, and these people, politically, have been a significant force in the whole of Nepal since that time. As was stated in the last chapter, the Khas were of Indo-European origin and spoke one of the Aryan dialects[10] (while Magar and Gurung spoke Tibeto-Burmese). Their economy was based mainly on pastoralism and animal breeding, but in every other respect they were similar to other hill people. In fact the text of the *Manusmriti, Dharmashastra* (Code of Conduct) treated and described the Khas in exactly the same way as the Tibeto-Burmese speaking Mongoloid peoples such as Gurung, Magar and other Kirat groups. Khas and Kirat are mentioned together, along with Dravida, Darada, Shaka and so forth, and are said to have become lower status by not observing the rules prescribed by Brahmins (*Manusmriti*, X: 43-44). But the recently Chhetrized Khas were led to believe that they were caste Hindus and had Rajput background. The Khas people who settled in the Kathmandu Valley and helped develop the caste code in the nineteenth century under Jung Bahadur's leadership did not realize that their ancestors in the western hills had come into contact with the stratified caste principle in the sixteenth century, little earlier than other ethnic groups living in the areas east of them.

Real confusion among the Khas began from the sixteenth century, after some of the powerful families took the title Thakuri along with the caste status of Chhetri and other less powerful yet ambitious and pretentious families assumed the title of Chhetri, wore the ritual thread, and became the clients of Bahun priests. Every ruling prince, of whatever ethnic background, took the title Thakuri around this time (Sharma, Janak Lal, 1982: 83). Also around this time, pundits began to circulate the idea that the term Khas meant fallen, and this caused irreparable and incalculable damage to the spirit of integrity and pride of the Khas people. Thakuri and the newly converted Chhetri began to despise their own kinsmen and the common people began to feel ashamed of being Khas. Any successful Khas or Magar began to conceal their background and isolate themselves from their own people, not only by assuming the title of Chhetri but also by commissioning the priests to create fictitious genealogies relating them to the plains people of India rather than to their own people. Once connected with the Rajputs in India they would be viewed as having been created for the purpose of ruling by the god himself. By inference, therefore, anyone who was not a convert himself into Chhetrihood and did not have a genealogy to prove the pedigree was not worthy to be the ruler. Consequently, the proud and mighty Khas, who had maintained their own state and identity for about 1200 years, beginning from the third century, and who had commanded one of the largest empires in the history of the entire Himalaya region for four hundred years, ended by becoming the much despised Matwali alcohol-drinking caste (See Pokhrel, 1974; Adhikari, 1988). At this later stage, some of these Matwalis, reluctant to identify themselves as Khas, attempted to call themselves Chhetri and Thakuri but others would not allow them to assume the title without the qualifying adjective Matwali. Consequently, there are large numbers of Matwali Thakuri and Matwali Chhetri in the far western region of the upper Karnali watershed today, while the Khas have vanished from the ethnographic map of Nepal (Sharma, 1971:45-6).

Most of the aristocratic Khas commissioned Bahun priests to initiate them so that they could wear the sacred thread and take the title of Chhetri; others who either could not afford or did not care to pay the Bahun priests, and yet later coveted the title of Thakuri and Chhetri, gradually began to call themselves Matwali Thakuri and Matwali Chhetri, while the bulk of the Khas became simply Matwali. The same process was subsequently adopted by the aristocracies among the high altitude Bhote, Magars and Gurungs, who claimed the title of Thakuri for themselves, even though not all of them wear the thread today. The trend among such people with few exceptions among Buddhist Thakuris was to claim their origins in India.

### *The Northern Himalayan Region*

Except at very high and cold altidues there is noregion today where Bahun families have not settled and have not helped the local rulers to adopt the high caste status. But the cold climate and the ice-fed cold water is not congenial for Bahun rituals as these involve frequent bathing in fresh water, and cleansing the premise with it too. Partially for this reason Bahuns have not had the motivation to seek conversions in the high mountain areas. The ruling family and the nobility in Mustang, located in the high Himalaya region, are the only people who did not adopt Hindu high caste status. The local culture is too rich and colourful to abandon in favour of Hindu caste rituals, and the Raja of Mustang, with about a dozen other families who are his kin and affines, have only the family name and the status of Thākuri without the ritual thread and an accompanying Bahun priest.

The northern Himalayan region was always inhabited by people of Tibetan origin who were followers of the Tibetan form of Buddhism—Lamaism. Most of these people practice the oldest form of Lamaism, as they have always been remote from Lhasa, the capital of Tibet. In places such as Mustang and Dolpo can be found the oldest forms of Lamaism, including pre-Buddhist BonPo monasteries. Occasionally, however, an itinerant fugitive Lama of one of the later reformed sects would arrive in these remote areas and, gradually, the full range of Tibetan religious forms were represented there. With the dispersion of Tibetan Buddhists out of Tibet, a sizable community has been established in the Kathmandu Valley, so that Tibetan culture and Buddhist ideology is again having some impact on Nepal.

*The Terai*

The Terai of Nepal has a slightly different history because of variations in geographic and ecological conditions compared to the hills. Apart from the most recent migrations, the majority of the Terai people are indigenous. The Tharu, Rajbansi, Koche, Meche, Dhimal, Satar, Danuwar and the Dhangars have always been there. Tharus are the most numerous among them. None except the Rajbansi and the Maithili people seem to have followed the hierarchic Hindu religion until the migration of the caste Hindus from the southern plains into the area during the nineteenth century. All of them therefore continue to practice primitive animism: worshipping spirits and many different objects or phenomena. Some of the Tharus have shamans or medicine men and healers called 'Guruva' while others only have ordinary spirit mediums and healers. The Rajbansi (meaning 'belonging to royal lineage') adopted Brahmanic forms of Hinduism during the medieval period. Originally these people were called the Koche, but adopted their new name which was meant to make them equivalent to Rajput in status. Other Koche adopted Islam.

Today there are three distinct cultures practising three different religions in the Terai plains of Nepal. There are the Hindus of the plains with caste groups intact, who are mostly found in eastern Terai districts of Saptari, Siraha, Mahottari, Dhanusha, Sarlahi, and Rautahat. Morang, Jhapa, and Chitwan were full of indigenous people until recently, but these are now outnumbered by immigrants from the hills. The entire western region was dominated by indigenous people like the Tharu until quite recently, when the hill people began to move down. Most of these indigenous people practice Shamanistic religious traditions privately, while accepting Hinduism in public, especially in attending festivals. The third group of people who have moved into parts of the Terai are the Islamic Mussulmans, who have been there from the middle of the nineteenth century.

In all Nepal, caste divisions and stratification are most pronounced among caste Hindus in the districts of eastern Terai. Most caste groups are found in these districts and therefore society there can be said to function according to the established principles of caste. The eastern Terai, particularly from Rautahat to Saptari, is dominated politically by high caste people who are rich and powerful. The poor lower castes form the majority but are dominated by these high castes, being dependent on them for their livelihood. However, recently, the increasing investment in construction projects and the development of an industrial infrastructure has created more jobs for the poor in the Terai, severing their dependence on the high-caste landowners. Such decreasing economic dependence forebodes a social and political independence as well, so that the future of the caste system in this area is increasingly in doubt.

### *The Eastern Hills*

The eastern hills, which largely comprise the Kirat area, were not hierarchized because the Bahuns did not arrive in the area until much later than their appearance in the Kathmandu Valley and the regions to the west. They began to trickle through only after the reunification of the Kirat region with the rest of Nepal. Most of the Kirats east of Sunkoshi river— namely the Jimi, the Rai, the Yakha, the Hayu, the Jirel, the Thami, and the Limbu—practice their own religion with their own gods and goddesses, priests and spirit mediums. Their various gods remained in ascendence even after the introduction of Hindu deities.

Among the Kirats of the eastern hills most influenced by the caste system, because of their proximity to Kathmandu, are the Sunuwars of Tamakosi valley. The Limbus are the least affected by the caste system because of their geographical distance. In the far east, the Bahuns themselves were much influenced by the independent-natured Limbu. The Bahuns of Pallo Kirat behaved very differently from their counterparts in the western hills and the Maithili area of the eastern Terai. In the west of Nepal, the migrant Brahmins wanted to preserve their faith and ritual practice in the Karnali basin—for them there was the matter of the survival of their culture. The persistent strategy of the Bahuns was to attach themselves to the local aristocracy whom they wooed with concocted genealogies. But an aristocracy is not a characteristic of the social organization of the Kirati groups in the east, which were tribal egalitarian groups, so that the Bahuns were less able to establish any kind of footing in Kirati society. Instead, in the Kirati mind the Bahuns represented an attempt at political and cultural intrusion by the Kathmandu authorities and were resisted as a politically subversive force (Caplan 1970). Further, by the time Bahuns entered the Kirat region they had been greatly secularized; their beliefs diluted with local hill traditions, and their ritualistic discipline relaxed. Not all Bahuns could find a living functioning in the capacity of priests and this forced a considerable modification in their lifestyle. They appear to have become more pragmatic and future-oriented, and less fatalistic. It has become almost impossible to find an orthodox Bahun in the entire Mechi zone. Local Shamans, priests, and spirit mediums continue to have a stronger influence than Bahun priests over the local people.

*Caste Flexibility and the Caste Panchayat*

The caste structure is not as impermeable as it is sometimes thought to be. It is possible, over several generations, to improve one's caste status. The untouchables cannot change their status as a group. However, there are always ways available for individuals to change caste status, by means of acquiring education, economic prosperity, and political support. It also requires that the individual remain isolated from other members of the low caste group, so that they must be strong enough to withstand the social pressure to conform and stay in the caste of origin, as well as that social pressure from the targeted group to remain low caste. Few survive these double pressures without becoming strongly alienated from society as a whole, and the personal cost has been great.

The situation at the other end is similarly rigid. No Bahun is allowed to practise a priestly job once caste status is lost through prohibited behaviour. But this does not exclude them from high status secular positions in economic and political life. The Bahun community has very little leverage in imposing sanctions against the unorthodox behaviour of any member of their caste—the caste panchayats are simply not strong enough. Individuals even in rural areas enjoy much greater freedom compared to their counterparts in similar situations in India. Generally speaking, caste regulations in Nepal have never been applied strictly because there have never been sufficient numbers of the Bahun community who have been assertive, except in exclusively Maithili speaking Hindu caste communities in the east central Terai districts.

Many Bahuns, particularly in the outer regions with little history of hierarchic caste practices have lapsed into unorthodoxy. For example, it is common in these areas for Bahuns to marry either across caste, or in an irregular manner (marrying divorcees, capture marriages, etc.). The offspring of these irregular marriages and of those who otherwise have been judged 'impure', are known as Jaishi. The offspring of mixed marriages, while being of Chhetri status, retain their father's family name. Consequently, there is a much larger number of people with Bahun family names in Nepal than there are pure (Upadhyaya) Bahuns. Since Bahun ethical norms do not restrict the Jaishi in any way, they manage to be far more competitive in the real world of politics and business than the pure Bahuns.

Caste systems are more marked by exceptions than by their rules in the Kathmandu Valley and the Jyapus are the best example of this. They have never observed strict caste rules, even though regulations promulgated in the fourteenth century classified them as low caste Shudras. Yet some of the rituals dependent on their service traditionally use them in a way that it would be considered polluting if the caste system were strictly observed. For example, they have the responsibility of carrying many sacred ritual objects at important festivals in Kathmandu—which in India would be considered defiling behaviour with serious consequences. Without Jyapus, there would be very few ritual ceremonies and festivals, and the Matsendra chariot, the Kumari, Bhairab, and the Ganesh chariot, during Indra Jatra, would not be carried around the cities of Patan and Kathmandu.

Newar society is structurally complex with many different caste groups, but they fail to observe rigid principles of cleavage and vertical hierarchy. There is no caste group solidarity anywhere comparable to that existing in parts of India, which is maintained through the functioning of caste panchayats, or councils. Whatever socially regulative councils were operative among the Newar originated before the introduction of the caste system and have a professional or trade basis. Caste panchayats do exist elsewhere in Nepal, but their power is inconsiderable. Typically, each caste has a caste panchayat, including the untouchables. Caste panchayats are councils of elders who come together to adjudicate or settle intra-caste disputes or make judgements concerning violation of proper caste behaviour, e.g., breaking caste taboos or violating the marriage rules in unequal caste relations. Though its functions are mainly judicial, the caste panchayat is not integrated into the formal legal system. If a determination is challenged, then an appeal is made to the district courts. Village councils (which are sometimes called panchayat) also fill these general judicial functions. In some areas there were both caste councils and village councils. This is true of the caste villages, found mostly in the Terai. In the hills, in the ethnic communities there are no caste councils; just village councils.

Decisions in these councils are based on local tradition, and older people are preferred as members because they have the greatest experience and knowledge of these traditions. There is no use of physical punishment in the Hindu system and no form of incarceration for the convicted offender. Instead, punishment consists of loss of caste status, ostracism, fines, or the offender is granted forgiveness (which is a sanction to the extent that it involves humiliation as the offender must admit to the offence, throw himself on the mercy of the council, and then thank the council for their leniency).

For everyone who is committed to the caste system, other than the untouchable, the greatest sanction is the threat of loosing caste status. Social ostracism is another form of punishment meted out by the caste panchayat and this can be particularly devastating in a village society. To survive in a village agricultural community cooperation is often essential for ploughing, harvesting, or building. To be socially ostracized is in effect a form of social death that must result in extreme hardship to the offender. Fines are the least powerful punishment in the caste areas, and typically involve very small amounts. Such fines are, again, essentially a form of humiliation, and their payment an admission of the misdeed.

When caste status is lost, the typical response is for the offender to migrate to some totally new area and to pass as a member of a desired caste. Passing is not restricted to the fugitive from the caste panchayat, but is a widespread practice in Nepal. People even attempt to pass as Bahuns, which is manageable as long as they do not pretend

### *Decreasing Significance of Caste*

Though the caste system does not have any official recognition at the State level, there are quite a few people at higher levels who see benefits in maintaining the structure. In an attempt to revitalize the caste system they have been trying to use the privileged position of the King to have caste legitimated in an indirect way. In the coronation ceremony of His Majesty, King Birendra, in 1975, pro-caste elements contrived to have the King anointed by a Bahun, Chhetri, Vaishya and Shudra. For this purpose a Limbu was nominated as a Shudra and a Shrestha as a Vaishya. This gave cause for alienation to a large section of the Shrestha and Limbu population who were insulted to be placed in these low status roles. It was a political mistake, for it may have flattered the egos of a few orthodox pundits trying to impose caste attitudes but it did not convince the majority of the Newars and the ethnic communities of their respectable place in Nepali society. Subsequently, some priests initiated four boys of another Kirat group, the Rais, into Chhetri status (Acharya, Laxm, 1986). This act of initiating Kirat boys into Chhetri status is in total contradiction with the earlier act of treating a Limbu, another Kirat group, as Shudra. These are typical examples of the expedient behaviour Nepali society has been subjected to in recent years.

The caste system of Nepal has always been unique and not copied something from abroad. The reason is that it had to adapt and adjust to a socio-cultural system with a very different background. Some of those who accepted the caste system and its accompanying belief system succumbed to the tendency to reorient away from Nepali society towards India, and developed a belief that India was a superior culture. Indian Hinduism was taken as the ideal. Recently, as the Indian Hindu upper class itself becomes less attached to caste, this Indian alienation from caste has been echoed among high class people in Nepal as well. Those who have travelled outside of south Asia have broadened their perspective and appreciate the limited and archaic nature of caste. The abolition of caste laws (differential punishment for offenders of different castes for the same offence), in 1963, has done much to change the attitude of the people towards the caste structure.

### *Caste and Ethnicity*

The Thakuri, Chhetri and Matwali people in the far western hills of Nepal are not divided rigidly by caste cleavages. Economic or political considerations tend to divide people rather than caste distinctions. All the major groups of people eastward from the far west are defined ethnically rather than by caste, such as Magar, Tharu, Gurung, Thakali, Sherpa, Tamang, Sunuwar, Thami, Rai, Limbu, Danuwar, Dhimal, etc. Increasing agitation by pundits in support of the nation-wide extension of the caste system has had a direct influence on consolidating the ethnic identity of these various groups within Nepali society. This increased sense of ethnic solidarity is a result of the defensive reaction against the intrusive and dominating activities of the Bahun-Chhetri. The various groups of people who do not have caste groupings have no way of maintaining group solidarity other than through their ethnic groups. This leads to the emphasis on ethnic identity.

Ethnic Matwali groups are aware that once they identify themselves as Hindus they will be placed at a low social status and will be at a disadvantage. As a result we are beginning to see the assertion of ethnic organizations for political and economic rights. There has been some exploitation of this ethnic dissatisfaction by political activists and some members of the various ethnic groups are rallying under the slogan of ethnic rights to fight the high caste Hindu domination. But this development is not unique to Nepal. It is quite common where ethnic minorities feel that they have been discriminated against. Clifford Geertz, who observed this particular phenomena in areas around the world, states that it is the manifestation of a 'desire to be recognised as responsible agents whose wishes, acts, hopes and opinions matter and it is the desire to build an efficient, dynamic modern state; it is a search for an identity, and a demand that the identity be publicly acknowledged as having import, a social assertion of the self as being somebody in the world'(Geertz, 1973)[11].

Many Nepali intellectuals are beginning to echo the same opinion, as will be clear if we look at the viewpoint expressed by Prayag Raj Sharma. He suggests that 'a new basis of national integration will have to be found to give the country a new strength of unity... Our true search should be to continue to find harmony in group relationship, but the values on which they are to be based must be compatible with the time' (Sharma, 1986).

Within Kathmandu, social relations between the dominant caste groups and ethnic minorities are complex. As will be fully elaborated in later chapters, social life in the capital is greatly influenced by key caste values and interpersonal styles, and prominent among these is the requirement of membership in appropriate social groups that are called afno mannche. For one to make any kind of social progress or get things done, one must have the correct afno mannche connections. These afno mannche connections are not necessarily caste based, but membership to them takes time, knowledge, and the right kind of support elsewhere. These resources are rarely available to the ethnic minority member newly arrived in Kathmandu from some remote region, and hence this kind of person will always tend to be excluded from an effective social and political life there. This is not so much a matter of discrimination because of membership of an ethnic minority group, or because of low caste status, but is a form of social exclusion in the absence of other qualifications necessary for group membership. Ethnic minorities, then, are disadvantaged and excluded in Kathmandu by default.

Ethnic minority members attempting to make their way into the modern world also are prone to experiencing special forms of acculturation. As will be seen in the chapter on education, ethnic minority families are typically very poor and dependent on their children's labour for survival, and cannot afford the luxury of sending them to school—which tends to be reserved for upper caste or upper class children. Those that do get an education are therefore from elite families. Ethnic minority members who are able to go to graduate school tend to adopt high caste attitudes, as the permeability in the Nepali caste system offers the hopes of caste mobility. A hierarchic attitude is often developed, and part of the process essentially requires the rejection of low caste or ethnic background. As a consequence the ethnic community looses the ambitious and mobile, who still have a long way to go to be accepted in a higher caste, and which may be possible only for descendants. The ethnic minority member is, therefore, in some kind of social and existential vacuum, having tenuous, repressed connections with ethnic antecedents and a dubious position within the caste society of the capital. The high caste attitude at that point provides the only immediate and even remotely accessible social reality, which again forces the individual into reorienting to a hierarchic caste perspective. As an objective the higher status will always be unattainable. A consequence is often the eventual breakdown of the defence mechanism of the ethnic individual, with demonstration of erratic behaviour and a loss of motivation. Few ethnic Matwalis are successful, and even when this is so they often have frustrated, bitter, and difficult personalities.

Most turn their grievances into political activity of an essentially revolutionary kind.

The typical indices of failures in acculturation and ethnic conflict are largely obscured in Nepal. Delinquency is ignored or even not recognized. There is little awareness of the existence of mental illness, other than psychotic breakdowns. No generally useful statistics has been collected for measuring the pervasiveness and form of failures in acculturation. It is therefore difficult to examine the extent to which these different ethnic groups are prone to alienation and what the social cost of this alienation is to the nation. Though it is obscured, it is nonetheless there. To some extent, the absence of visible alienation and social conflict is consequent to the economic nature of Kathmandu, which does not have many industries and is really not seen as a place of opportunity, except for those who have administrative ambitions. Hence there is little urban drift to Kathmandu, and there is no developing slum area of rural migrants who have left their homes hoping for some opportunity to improve their lot. Kathmandu attracts mainly prosperous and upper class people. Those with economic ambitions among the various ethnic groups go to the Terai, or even to India. Becoming an expatriate is a common alternative for the frustrated but ambitious ethnic group member.

NOTES AND REFERENCES

1. The caste system was legalized for the entire country in the Code of 1854.
2. Brahmanism refers to that development beyond Vedic traditions based essentially in the Puranas, which heavily emphasizes fatalism through its stress on karmic determination, from which has developed the social organization of the varna or caste system.
3. Sometimes spelled Mashto, and, in the upper Karnali basin, Maitho.
4. The Khas people in the Kumaon hills beyond the western border of Nepal, in India, have a similar situation in relat- to Brahmanism (Majumdar, 1944).
5. To get around the significance of the merchant class in Newar society, they had to compromise by using the class

term Shrestha, meaning noble, to apply to the Newar merchants, placing them in a level of Kshatriya caste.

6. It is interesting that much earlier than Jung Bahadur, some Magars took the title of Rana. Today no-one takes seriously the suggestion that the Rana Magars are of Rajput origin because they did not succeed in securing power and wealth as was done by Jung Bahadur, his brothers and their descendants.
7. Due to a lack of historic sensitivity, some people continue to treat Newars as a seperate ethnic group without recognising their origins as the urbanized descendants of migrant groups from many different ethnic peoples of Nepal.
8. 'Taking an average for 1955-56 through 1960-61, the paddy yield per hectare of arable land in Japan was 4.56 and 2.54 tons in China (Ishikawa, 1967: 70) which is the highest in the world. Around the eighteenth century the paddy yield in the Kathmandu valley had already reached 3.9 tons per hectare (Hamilton, 1819: 225). Today the average yield of Bulu (one of the Jyapu settlements of the valley) is 4.3 tons per hectare' (Pradhan, 1981:9).
9. Vidya harae Kashi (Benaras) janu, insaaf harae Gorkha janu.
10. This Khas language came to be used as the lingua franca of the region west of Kathmandu from the fourteenth century, and through the entire country from the eighteenth century. The Nepali language is this Khas language. The adoption of Nepali as the national language later gave advantage to its native speakers, politically, at the cost of other, non-Nepali speaking people, including the Newar-speakers of the Kathmandu valley.
11. Geertz further suggests that there is no single established method or strategy that the minority people would adopt in order to make their point of view heeded. There are several ways of doing this. An extract from his text will make the point clear:

    When we speak of communalism in India, we refer to religious contrasts; when we speak of it in Malaya, we are mainly concerned with racial ones, and in the Congo with tribal ones. But the grouping under a common rubric is not simply adventitous; the phenomena referred to are in some way similar. Regionalism has been the main theme in Indonesian disaffection, differences in custom in Moraccan. The Tamil minority in Ceylon is set off from the Sinhalese majority by religion, language, race, region and social custom; the Shiite minority in Iraq is set off from the dominant Sunnis virtually by an intra-Islamic sectarian difference alone. Pan national movements in Africa are largely based on race, in Kurdistan, on tribalism; in Laos, the Shan States, and Thailand, on language. Yet all these phenomena, too, are in some sense of a piece(Geertz,ibid:256-257).

# CHAPTER THREE

# FAMILY STRUCTURE AND CHILDHOOD SOCIALIZATION

This brief chapter is a prelude to the succeeding one, detailing certain peculiarities of socialization that may be of interest in understanding personality characteristics and interpersonal styles, which have an effect on Nepal's response to development in the past forty years. It is only an overview of socialization practices, based on my own fieldwork, and attempts to briefly consider issues that are frequently addressed by cultural anthropologists. As a background to an examination of socialization practices, the chapter begins with a discussion of the nature of the family and the role of women in Nepali society.

Families in Nepal tend to be nuclear, except among a few upper class business families in Kathmandu and some land-owning families in the Terai who live in large joint families. In the absence of any security for old age, except for government employees, the elderly need to be looked after by their sons and daughters-in-law. Therefore it is quite common to find old people living with married sons. With these exceptions, the standard pattern for families tends to be husband, wife and their unmarried children, and this is true of the entire country. Presently, old age security and age-related problems of senility, loneliness and health care are largely taken care of within the family. Many people among the Hindu high caste families worry more about their next life than about old age and are interested in having as many sons as possible to maintain the ritualistic practices necessary for a successful afterlife. To ensure this many people continue to have children till they have one or more male offspring. There are cases where people with a large number of female children continue to have babies in the hope of having at least one male child. This affects their attitude towards family planning. Family planning has, therefore, been less effective among high caste Hindus than among low caste and other non-caste ethnic people in rural Nepal.

There is always a strong bond between the living and the dead in Nepal in the form of a reciprocal dependency. Ancestors are believed to be dependent on the living descendants and the living are dependent on the dead for a sense of security. Dead relatives are called pitri, the ancestors. People believe that they are dependent for their prosperity and welfare on their pitri, who are believed to take care of all inexplicable problems and prospects that people within the family may have. Thus, everyone tries to appease them and keep them happy by offering them the food that they think their pitri would like most. In many ways the ancestors become easier to handle and please since they do not interact directly with the living, and hence are not objects of interpersonal conflict. At the same time they reinforce self-assurance. There is, in fact, greater concern for dead relatives than for living ones. This also explains why there are no elaborate rituals for the dead who die young, before marriage, and without children. The elaborateness of the ritual is related to the dependence of juniors on the seniors who have more power and experience. If someone dies young, they do not have the experience and power that warrants particular attention.

Women in Nepal generally have equal status except among Bahun-Thakuri and some middle and upper level Chhetri. Since the population of such high caste people is not large the percentage of women who are underprivileged in comparison to men is relatively small. However, the educated and articulate section of women invariably come from among the high caste Hindus and tend to present the situation differently.

Women, like men, have specialized jobs. Even in agriculture there are differences in the jobs assigned to men and women while, in the domestic sphere, women hold more power and authority than their menfolk. Women remain tied to the home and this leads to the assumption that women enjoy less freedom than men in general. But there are many examples to show that women are treated as equal to men. The Newar women of Bulu (Pradhan, 1981), the Tharu women of Dang (Rajaure, 1981), the Kham Magar of Thabang (Molnar, 1981), the women of Baragaon (Schular, 1981), have been presented in the Status of Women Study Series showing that they are by no means treated as unequals. Similarly, equality and freedom among Rai women have been described by McDougal (1973); among the Limbus by Jones (1976); among the Sherpa by Furer-Haimendorf (1964); among the Rana Tharu of Kailali by Bista (1972) and among Tamang by Holmberg (1989). Women's specialized jobs are concerned with the maintenance of the house, the preparation and processing of food, and the care of the aged and the very young, all of which tend to keep them at home for long periods of time. This does not necessarily mean that they are less privileged than men as women are free to go anywhere, to attend fairs, festivals, wedding parties, make trade trips, and so forth. Women in rural areas, with little education, have been elected as panchayat members and, indeed, there have been few village panchayats that had a majority of women as their members.

For the high caste women, things are very different. The Hindu *Dharmashastras*, such as the *Manusmriti*, state that women should be under the strict control and supervision of their fathers until marriage, under the control of the husband after marriage, and that of a son after the death of the husband. A woman without one or other of these male supervisors lives inauspiciously and precariously. Supported by the principles of such disciplinary theories the high caste males justify themselves in limiting the freedom of their women. A high caste Hindu widow, therefore, cannot attend festive occasions like weddings and vrtabandha (initiation ceremonies). Orthodox Hindus consider it unlucky and inauspicious to see the face of a woman who is either widowed, without a male issue, or a spinster. For women of the Bahun caste there is a negative value attached to going outside for a walk, social call or for any other purpose than important work (Bennett, 1983). Therefore they get very little opportunity to socialize, and are not supposed to know too much or to gossip about their own neighbourhood. A woman who knows and talks too much is considered excessive and loose. An ideal woman is close-lipped and active in looking after the household (ibid). Such rules apply to the middle economic level Bahun, Chhetri and Shrestha Newars alone. The aristocracy and upper class ignore all such rules as they consider themselves above common rules and the poorer people in marginal rural areas cannot afford to observe many such stringent rules or are outside the bounds of caste behaviour.

Typically, marriages are arranged for high caste groups, though others aspiring to raise their status and prestige also mimic the practice. Such arranged marriages are successful in the case of Bahuns,in the sense that the marriages are not dissolved or replaced,but this is not the case for Chhetris, where the arranged marriage has a high tendency to fail. If the Chhetri male loses interest in his wife, he can always bring in another wife. If a Chhetri woman loses interest in her husband, she must elope. Hence women are the ones who make the decision to terminate a marriage more often than men. These arranged marriages are much less successful than the non-arranged ones, so that among the Chhetris of the rural area one finds the highest rate of elopement than any other group in Nepal.

Outside of these high caste groups there is no common practice of arranged marriage. Among the ethnic communities, what is common is called a capture marriage. In a capture marriage, the bride is.captured by the groom and his friends, and is whisked away into married life. This is now a mock event; bride and groom are usually girlfriend and boyfriend, and the bride's parents often conveniently absent themselves so as not to interfere with the capture. Being captured is highly desired by the young ethnic girl, as it demonstrates to her and to others that she has the qualities that warrant such an adventurous act on the part of the groom. Capturing can also be useful in terminating failed marriages when an alternative is available.

Prior to 1963 Bahuns married at earlier ages; for girls even as early as ten or eleven. The grooms could be of any age. Frequently a widowed Bahun even at the age of sixty or seventy married girls of ten or eleven years of age. This created a situation where quite a few Bahun women were widowed at an early age, sometimes before puberty and were forced by religious rules to remain as widows for the rest of their lives. Today there is a legal provision that girls cannot be married before sixteen, though in remote regions marriages still occur at slightly younger ages. In rural areas Bahun women now tend to marry at sixteen, while in developed urban areas the common age is closer to twenty. Other non-caste women might marry at any age, though the typical marriage age for girls is between seventeen to eighteen and that for boys between nineteen and twenty. Regardless of the age at marriage, women start to bear children right away.

In early days there was no limit to the number of wives that a man could have. The Bahun-Chhetri males tended to favour multiple wives. The Lama Buddhists in the high altitude practised fraternal polyandry, which was common among the Tibetans. Since 1963, monogamy has been mandatory.

The female members of every household have to work at least twelve to fourteen hours in an average day, seven days a week even when the male members of the same household lounge around or spend their days in gambling. They have to work on the farms, look after livestock and children, and attend to all the domestic chores, including cooking, cleaning, washing and processing food for cooking, such as husking, grinding and polishing grain. Mothering is a primary job for women, and there is much similarity in the nature of this task across caste and ethnic boundaries. Among the middle class modern educated these general practices are changing. As we shall see, there are also some significant caste differences. Typically a family will have four children. There is a high infant mortality rate, and this possibly affects parent-child relationships, both positively and negatively.

Breast feeding lasts until another child comes along; sometimes up to the age of four years or beyond. There is a weaning ceremony, when children are given solid foods or rice at the age of six or seven months, but this is just a ritual and mothers continue to allow their children to suckle as long as no other child is born. There is no toilet training at all, except that caste children do learn to use their left hand and not their right. Defecation and urination has little social regulation in Nepal, even in adulthood, so that people defecate in the streets with minimal privacy and little concern for what their action might mean for others.

Babies are carried on the mother's back, facing the mother and tied with a large band. The baby's arm movements are unrestricted in this position, with only the legs tied. At home, babies are free to crawl anywhere and young children are unrestricted in their play activities, except that Bahun children are not allowed into the kitchen until they have been initiated. Also, as soon as the Bahun child begins to move around they are kept away from lower caste children.

Corporal punishment is given sparingly, and mostly the mother punishes the child with the flat of the hand. Social isolation is not a common punishment for children, nor is there a threat of withdrawal of love. Other kinds of threats are used to persuade children to behave properly, particularly threat of the dark. For the child, the dark is peopled with imaginary evil. It is also common for mothers to curse their children and often swear at them. Curses include 'Death to you!', 'Why don't you die?' or invoke promises of vengeance, illness, and fatal disease. Women's swearwords usually make references to death or illness, while men tend to make sexual references. Aspersions on the child's competence is also often made in the form of accusations such as 'Aren't you stupid!' Bahuns, on the other hand, do not swear, and do not fight.

There is a strong sense of protection towards the child, and there are always grandparents, older siblings, uncles and aunts around to regulate the behaviour of the child. The child is generally indulged upon till the birth of another child. Toys are usually improvised and homemade, and are miniatures of what the adults use; pots and pans for girls and work tools for the boys. Little is kept from the child, and there are few sexual taboos.

A very close relationship exists between mother and child in the first four-year period. The mother washes the child, teaches it to behave properly, and administers punishment. Such a relationship becomes modified only by the advent of a younger sibling, who then receives the bulk of attention, or, if there is an older sibling, much of the child-rearing task is shifted to this sibling.

At four or five, the child begins to work and then starts its separation from the mother. It either has to look after a younger child, especially if female, or herd the family's sheep and goats. The child's task becomes that of driving the goats to the common village grazing grounds, which could be more than two kilometres away. The novice four-year old does not take up full responsibility for the goats and sheep to start off with, but follows the advice of an 'adult' in charge, meaning the eight- or ten-year old who trains the youngster. Children also start to play under the guardianship of the older siblings. Four-year-olds play improvised games, including marbles, water slides, 'soldiers and police', 'village court' where they make mock adjudications, and they play marriage. There are no organized games with competitive teams and complex rules.

As a rule there are no prohibitions on violent behaviour among children. Nevertheless, violent behaviour is not common. When it does happen the child is not specially reprimanded, but instead parents usually defend their own children regardless of what they have done. Quarrelling is usually verbal. Children are notoriously mischievous, and such mischievousness is actively encouraged by adults other than the parents, who see such behaviour as being particularly 'cute' or appealing. Children are thus often exposed to contradictory demands on behaviour, with parents encouraging them to behave in one manner, and other adults often encouraging them to behave in another. Such inconsistency eliminates any sense of the real appropriateness of behaviour, and undermines any genuine sense of authority. There is no moral pressure or guilt feeling regarding immoral acts, because there is little sense of morality instilled in children: a sense of social responsibility is simply not internalized and social sanctions are only effective in an external form. Only the fear of punishment discourages individuals from doing anything wrong. This is a significant reason why it is important to have many friends, relatives and supporters (as afno manchhe) in positions of importance, so that one can get away with irresponsible behaviour without being punished for it. But the failure to internalize social mores acts to increase the Nepali orientation to the outside, to intensify the dependency on the external,a fundamental aspect of Nepali character that will be considered in the next chapter.

Children of Bahun priests grow up committing fewer mischiefs than other children and this facilitates the development of a special regard for the priestly Bahun character in the village setting. Bahuns are generally seen to be more moral in their behaviour, and because of this can pass judgement over the activities of others, even in non-caste villages. The adverse consequence of this is that, encouraged by the general impression they make on others with regard to their moral behavior, Bahuns grow to adulthood being self-righteous but without an ability to be self-critical. They may make critical comments on the values and lifestyle of any other community or an ethnic group but cannot stand criticism of their own lifestyle.

The self-righteous attitude among the Bahun youths is having a direct repurcussion on the behaviour pattern of the non-caste ethnic youths recently. They are beginning to rebel against the hierarchic order of castes and ethnic groups. They want to be treated as equals,they want to be noticed and taken seriously. Since this does not come easily in a society which is dominated by hierarchic caste principles they are trying to show their unhappiness through violence and disregard of civic rules in public. There is an increasing tendency among such youths to try and assert their equal status through rude behaviour in public as well as in private life. By Bahunistic standards, politeness and courtesy is associated with low caste behaviour. At least this is how the increasingly urban oriented ethnic youths see it. Of course, all of this is being exacerbated with the increasing exposure of the Nepalis to the outside world. The influence of foreign aid, tourism and the bombardment of statistical interpretations showing Nepalis as the poorest and the most backward has done a great deal of damage to the positive qualities of the Nepalis in general. If Bahunism destroyed the self-esteem of the Nepalis vis-a-vis India in the past the currently expanding international modernism has pushed the Nepali youths all the way to the bottom of the global economic hierarchy in their own self-image. This has not helped to develop a positive attitude among many of them.

The close relationship between the mother and a male child continues until the child can become an assistant in the father's work. At about eight or nine the child becomes generally independent of the mother; by the time the child is fourteen it is separated from the mother. Characteristically, an excessive adulation develops for the father, based mostly on the observation of his activities connected with work. It is common to hear Nepali boys make great claims for their fathers, who assume almost superhuman dimensions. There are sayings which exemplify the image of a father for young children until their late teens. When children attempt to show off in such adventures as tree climbing, jumping over chasms, or wading across rivers, if their feat becomes difficult or impossible, they start bragging about their fathers being the only people in the world who could perform this action. They believe that fathers can do everything. Very few children are taught to compete or to try and achieve better than their fathers. Fathers symbolize the ultimate in achievement. Besides assisting the father, goat tending continues until the child becomes a usable adult labourer, between fourteen and sixteen, by which time he becomes a full time member of the labour force, and is often considered old enough to marry.Until the fifties children of the Rana and other upper class families grew up being surrounded by maids, male escorts and servants but usually without any attendant tutors or governesses. This tended to spoil rather than educate them. Family background rather than personal achievement has thus been emphasized in the process of socialization for the children.

There is no concept of children as a separate section of Nepali society. In fact, in a large part of the country and in a majority of cases, there is no point at which children cease to be children and become adults. The only exception to this is that the Bahuns, Chhetris, Vajracharyas, Sakya Bhikshus, Chhathare and Panchthare Shresthas, and the twice born castes among the Terai Hindus, have a practice of initiation, the Vrtarabandha, or the sacred thread-wearing ceremonies. For the most part, life is a single continuum with no apparent disjuncture between childhood, youth and adulthood. In Nepal such distinctions are not made in the same way as elsewhere. For example, there is no area that adults think is inappropriate for children. As already indicated, most children grow up learning about sex at an early age and few grow up without knowing the sexual activities of the adults. Many children play mock sexual intercourse at a very early age. As small or immature adults, children are more likely to have the rights and the responsibilities of adulthood, particularly the responsibilities of contributing to the economic sustenance of the family. As such they are expected to work early and, in many cases, are needed as workers for the survival of the family. Families often cannot afford the luxury of letting their children have the time off to attend school, let alone pay for an incidental expense associated with an education. For these reasons education is not viable, and is ignored by many in the rural ethnic areas.

Dependence on parents is much higher and continues for a much longer period among Nepalis, as compared to other people around the world. In fact, many Nepalis continue to rely on their parents throughout their lives and never become independent. There is no institution, value system, or education to wean anyone away from parents at any age. Some among the young try to be independent, at least economically, from their parents because it is considered good and desirable by modern standards. This is becoming increasingly important for women as well who have been educated and want to enjoy freedom from the traditional domination of males and of the senior females of their husband's family after marriage. But there has not been much evidence of educated women weaning their husbands away from the dependent psychology which men develop towards their parents at an early age. A man could be strongly influenced by his wife for all kinds of reasons and for many practical purposes; but his dependency, deep inside, upon his parents rarely diminishes. People at any level of society and within any ethnic, caste or linguistic group, are never taught to be independent from their parents. A man may be very successful, but is not expected to be independent ritually, socially or psychologically. Many traditional rituals have to be conducted by fathers or older siblings, even after everyone within the family has achieved adulthood and economic self-sufficiency. The importance of fathers, specially among upper class families, does not diminish as long as they live. Until 1950 the Rana government did not recognise any personal talent, ability or academic qualifications except proper parentage. Important positions were held by the sons of important fathers regardless of the capabilities of the incumbent candidate.

The tradition of primogeniture among the British and Japanese may have helped in developing a strong and conservative cultural tradition through the first born and a very adventurous, competitive and independent attitude among junior siblings. The Nepali tradition of equal distribution of property among all male children and of a protective and patronizing attitude towards junior children, especially the youngest, helped develop the dependency syndrome to the extreme. Beyond personal inclination and compatibility, there is no preferential treatment or expectation between specific male children either by law or tradition. Therefore, children usually compete for paternal attention and a share of paternal property.

In most cases, the young men stop depending on their fathers if they find an alternative father figure to look after them. This can be one of many possibilities. The Gorkha soldiers, for example, develop this dependency on their superior officers in the British army. In another situation the poor and helpless address and consider their patron or mentor as a father figure. It is common to address the king as the father of the nation,which is not the same thing as saying, in the western sense, the founding fathers or city fathers; nor can it be compared to the biological relationship. In case of separation or the death of the father, a mother takes charge of minor children only if there are no male members in the household of the deceased. In Nepal, if a marriage breaks down it is always the father who takes care of children and never the mother.

In most cases, when growing up, children are kept busy assisting their parents. Usually there is a certain degree of gender differentiation, in the sense that boys tend to assist their fathers and the girls help their mothers with chores in the kitchen, washing, laundering and in taking care of junior siblings. Though they are socialized at an early age to assume gender-appropriate adult role behaviour, the Nepali youth are remarkably free from restraint in any form. This is not the case with Bahun children, especially, in a priestly family.

While growing up, the Bahun child in a priestly family is taught that he is the cleanest or most pure, the best, the elite, the closest to god, with special spiritual qualities. But they are also taught that these qualities are fragile, and can be easily compromised through the introduction of pollution. Pollution, then, is something which they learn to fear at an early stage.And the sources of pollution are the great bulk of the people around them.The child of a priest cannot participate in singimg, dancing, playing,or sports,and must stay away from the other children. In today's secular context and school activities such children are encouraged by their parents to only recite poems and make speeches while most other children participate in dancing, singing and in competitive sports as well where socialization takes place among children of different caste and ethnic backgrounds. If some kind of injury is done to the children of the priestly families, they cannot retaliate, not only because violence is not an option for them, but because retaliation might require physical contact, and this can lead to pollution. They are consequently fearful of possible hostility which makes them appear timid.

Priests cannot work, because work is a low caste occupation. Though their boys will go and tend goats, sheep and cattle, they will never begin a work apprenticeship in a productive field. Instead they will be taught by their fathers to be literate in Sanskrit, and will be taught the ritual activities of their priestly calling. Options other than that of priesthood are slim, and other administrative jobs can come by only if the family is favourably positioned with people in authority. Apart from that the Bahun priests often face a very precarious economic existence, which they cannot ameliorate through casual labour. Consequently one often finds them in poverty. This constant threat of poverty also adds to their sense of insecurity. This strong sense of insecurity makes them constantly unhappy and nagging in temperament. In a survey conducted by a sociologist among people of various caste and ethnic backgrounds in the Chitwan district it was found that the Bahuns were the unhappiest of all; many Tharus and Boteys were much poorer in economic resources but were reported to be more satisfied with life(Bhandari, 1986).

It is within these contradictions that the youth in a priestly family, although isolated and highly insecure, must grow to be an elite. They are always a minority, because once their population in a particular village expands, there are not enough clients to go around and they have to split and move on. Their original background is one of expulsion, of fleeing the Islamic Jihad to preserve a unique and endangered lifestyle. So there is a long history of movement and a strong sense of being continually displaced. They are taught from the earliest age that they are different and that they must maintain this difference. They develop a certain sense of isolation, which is accompanied by a sense of alienation and insecurity.But this is not at all true of the ethnic Bahuns who are not preoccupied with ritual purity or with exclusive caste related professions.

The child's socialization centres on the appreciation of caste distinctiveness, and the strongest concern becomes that of loss of caste status. Yet special problems arise for the high caste child as a consequence of the fact that orthodoxy is not rigidly maintained by all high caste families throughout Nepal. There is a large and developing discrepancy between the ideals of behaviour and actual manifestations. Threatened with the deep fear of pollution, the child of a priest often witnesses Bahun adults engaging in polluted or otherwise caste inappropriate behaviour. When a Bahun child, reared on the purity of his caste, discovers a father or close relative privately violating such behaviour, then he comes to share a deep and wicked secret about high caste life, that it masks a certain degree of fraudulence; that the high ideals of purity are often something of a public facade; and the sense of superiority is largely undeserved. In sharing this secret pollution of the Bahuns as a caste, the individual then develops a secondary concern, that it will be found out. Unlike the non-Bahun child, then, the Bahun does develop a certain inner psychological dynamic that involves guilt. Rather than motivating responsible behaviour, however, one of the consequences of this guilt is a deep and widespread paranoia, that has adverse effects in high caste social organization. This will be discussed in the next chapter.

There is one final special difference between the high caste member and other Nepalis. The latter is only gradually weaned from the mother, who always enjoys a respected position and the love of her children. This is not the case with the high caste male child. He, too, is suckled by his mother, and develops for her the same close attachment as found with any small child. But the mother as a woman is only a second class human being who, in spite of her high caste, is believed to have certain qualities that are also polluting. At an early age the male child is taken away from his mother and is encouraged to redirect his attachment to the father, who provides not only instrumental support in teaching what are considered as professional skills, but who also provide much of the expressive support as well. Further, while family relations in the typical Nepali family are very democratic, with the wife participating on an equal footing with the husband and where family decisions are taken together, in the high caste family, relations are patriarchal and decisions taken only by the husband or father. Females are subservient to males, and soon the mother is subject to the demands of her male children, particularly as they grow older. The high caste child, then, is never exposed to cooperative or democratic action, but knows only a social order of stratification and authoritarianism. This stratification becomes their only source of a sense of stability and certainty in a threatening world of differences and insecurity. Any threat to the caste system must be a deep personal threat that challenges their most basic sense of who they are. Resistance to any attempted change in the caste system, then, is motivated not simply by a favoured ideology, but by a defensive reaction to what is perceived as an attack on the self. This is the reason that caste related practices persist in many areas of social activity even after more than twenty-five years of its abolition officially and legally.

There are also special differences in socialization for the children of mixed Bahun-Matwali marriages, the source of most of those in the Chhetri caste. Reference has already been made to the special regard given to the kitchen in the Bahun household, and that children are kept away from it until initiated into their caste. In a mixed household things are more complicated. Typically, the father will be Bahun and the mother Matwali. The kitchen will be divided into various sections, with lines clearly demarcating their boundaries. These sections locate the areas where members of the various caste may or may not move. To violate the section boundaries is to pollute the kitchen, which then requires that special intensive cleansing rituals be performed before the kitchen can be brought back into use. The mixed household may include at least three castes, if not more, having wives from the Bahun, Chhetri, and Matwali castes, who must remain restricted to their appropriate areas. The father, then, eats in a separate area from the children, who eat in a separate area from the mother. Other areas of the house, especially the household sanctuary, are similarly restricted areas. The family is thus strongly divided along caste lines.

The mother, here, is even more disparaged than in the purely Bahun family. She is Matwali; not only a source of potential pollution, but the cause for the lowered, Chhetri, status of the son of the Bahun. In many family activities, she is ritually separated from her children at an early age. Among the more established Chhetri community, the new Chhetri faces exclusion and ridicule due to the immediacy of his Matwali background, and there are those who will treat this new Chhetri as lower. The Matwali background of the mother, therefore, is often denied, and the mother rejected to preserve status. This serves to compound the tendency to paranoia discussed in relation to the socialization of other high caste children.

The mixed Chhetri child, however, at the level of economic self-sufficiency, does enjoy certain benefits that other children do not. In particular, he will be educated by his father, and hence prepared for a high status life, generally in some administrative capacity.

CHAPTER FOUR

# VALUES AND PERSONALITY FACTORS

In examining Nepal's ability to adapt to technological and cultural change we need to consider not only those cultural values and social institutions that may facilitate or impede adaptation, but also certain characteristics of the Nepali people themselves: their motivation, cognitive abilities, and interpersonal styles. For instance, the study of modernization in Japan has been facilitated by considering the achievement motivation factor. Japan, however, when compared to Nepal, is a relatively homogeneous society. Nepal is multi-ethnic, and this multiplicity in culture parallels a multiplicity in psychological styles.

The emphasis in this book is on that section of Nepali society that currently positions itself as the main intermediarybetween Nepal's heteronomous society and the 'modern world'. This segment is that of the Bahun-Chhetri-Newaṛ, and those few among other ethnic groups that have adopted their particular Hindu hierarchic world view during the past couple of centuries. This chapter will make observations on the salient personality characteristics of this segment of society. These personality characteristics will, at places, be contrasted with those found elsewhere in Nepali society, but a more comprehensive examination of personality factors in these other areas of Nepal must await some other treatment, elsewhere. It must be emphasized that the emergent hierarchic subculture being examined here is a minority and is not representative of all the Nepali people. However, it is the most powerful subculture and presently determines the pace and character of Nepal's assimilation into the modern world.

## *The Sense of Causality and Fatalism*

Most Nepalis of the present generation, essentially from the Chhetri and Bahun castes, have been brought up according to a belief system that posits that one's circumstances have been determined by a supreme deity; that their lives have been fated. If one is happy and successful, it is because one must have earned this in a previous life. This is called *karma*. Karma literally means action, but in every day use people do not relate karma to their actions in the present life or in a previous one. The role of one's own personal actions in influencing karma is neglected and, instead, karma is thought to be predestined and as something which cannot be altered in any way. There is a practice of keeping red ink and a pen, along with a few other ritual objects, in a room where the mother sleeps with her new born baby on the sixth night after it is born. The popular belief, supported by the priests, is that on this sixth night, Bhavi, the demi-god of providence, comes to the house to write the fate of the child on its forehead. Thereafter, one's life is guided at all times by the writing of Bhavi and it is not possible to really alter one's *bhagya*, fate, by any deed unless it is of a ritualistic kind aimed at affecting powerful supernatural forces. Sometimes people show a human skull with its zigzag lines and furrows on the cranium, and claim that this is the alphabet of Bhavi.

Many poor Nepalis have a habit of cursing themselves, using the edge of their flattened hand, as if it were a knife, to hit their forehead, to express their frustrations over failures, miseries and sufferings. They continue to believe that 'one can have only what is written (on the forehead) but can not have what one sees' (*lekheko matrai painchha, dekheko paidaina*). Under these circumstances individuals are readily induced to accept powerful external forces as prime movers in the world.

### *Fatalism and Achievement Motivation*

Fatalism greatly affects purposeful problem-solving and goal-achievement behaviour. If the course of events is already determined then it makes little sense to attempt to independently influence their outcome. Personal effort might have some long term consequence, but only if it has some resonance at supernatural levels and only within parameters set by a supernatural decree. Consequently, the only kind of action that can influence one's destiny are those with religious merit. The model for such behaviour is provided by the Bahun priests, so that the traditional activities of the Bahun pundits are idealized as those most associated with future success. Prayer is open to all, but, as prescribed by the *Manusmriti*, only initiated Bahun pundits can function as priests. However, other Bahun activities are being opened to the lower castes; in particular, the learned activities of reading, writing, and engaging in debate. By emulating these activities low caste members often anticipate receiving the social benefits of high caste, and eventual identification with high caste status. Being educated, then, has a superstitious connection with high caste, and the advantage of being treated by supernatural powers as a Bahun.

Education is not looked upon as an act of acquiring intellectual powers or technical skills but is another form of ritualistic behaviour. On being educated the worldview of some students may be modified, and acculturation may support the development of genuinely instrumental ideas. But this is not the common response to education in Nepal, and regardless of the level of education attained, fatalistic-hierarchic ideas remain the core that determine the behaviour of the individual. Verses 19-23, chapter IV, of the *Bhagavad Gita* eloquenty emphasize the discipline of freeing oneself from desire, purpose and any instrumental action; and the *Bhagavad Gita* is very highly regarded by all high caste Hindus.

The most important focal constructs in understanding possible limitations in the Nepali attitude to development are those of achievement motivation and the work ethic, which here will be considered coextensively. Achievement motivation has been of primary interest to anthropologists and sociologists in studying social change in east Asia. Ruth Benedict tried to compare the Japanese source of motivation with that of the western Christian societies and attributed a sense of guilt to the Christian and a sense of shame to the Japanese as the primary motivational forces behind their respective work ethics (Benedict, 1946). By contrast, DeVos believes that guilt is still the primary factor at the base of Japanese achievement motivation (DeVos, 1973). Hindu high caste society tends to lack such mechanisms, which are not fostered by its ideologically fatalistic environment, and the attitude towards work is quite different.

Under this Hindu system, which is stratified and fatalistic, one has to engage in activities that are appropriate to one's caste. Those whose fate it is to be workers continue to work, but this work does not necessarily lead to any form of result or reward. The caste principle admonishes that actions have to be without desire, i.e. without a goal. There is a purpose to action, but it is a purpose known only to a supernatural agency. Individual aspirations are inconsequential and behaviour is submissive to a controlling force that is unknown.

Learned Hindus emphasize that the material world is *maya*, an illusion, and claim that this is not worth taking seriously. Poverty and deprivation are made bearable with a promise of a better rebirth. Priests even tell the poor and suffering that they are the chosen ones of God; that God wished them to remain poor so that they could remain devoted to Him. Prosperity is often interpreted as corruption. Once people get used to poverty and deprivation in this manner, they are not interested in working harder than is necessary for their subsistence. In any case, there is no dignity in labour. High caste people have always despised physical labour and are accustomed to believing, as well as teaching others to believe, that erudition and ritual are the only important things. They believe that material wealth and prosperity are the concern of the vulgar and low. Today's intellectual elite, therefore, consider it fashionable to condemn or despise anyone who achieves either position or prosperity through personal industry, just as they would condemn a criminal for being anti-social.

According to Sankhya philosophy, everything in this world is painful. All pleasure is accompanied by the fear of losing it. One begins to experience pain even before losing pleasure. So pleasure is impossible via material means. Wise men must reject all material things as they only perpetrate pain and misery; thus, they must abandon all materially purposeful self-gratifying action in favour of self-negation. Ideally, total renunciation involves relinquishing egotism and the cultivation of a state of meditation. At a popular level, even amongst illiterate people, any kind of work is equated with pain (*dukkha*) and people consider it an act of wisdom to avoid work. The opposite of dukkha is *sukkha* (bliss) which means living without having to work. People who can live without having to work are considered fortunate. As a career objective in modern Nepal, every Nepali tries to have a Jagir, a salaried job where one does not have to work but will receive a pay cheque at the end of each month. Candidates still show their zeal and enthusiasm for work at the time of applying for the job, because that is the rule one has to follow. But in such jobs one is not expected to actually work.

By contrast, low caste people have always been hard workers, and have been forced to develop very high levels of endurance. When opportunities arose, they found that hard work led to economic success. Therefore, in most areas of Nepal, low caste people are fast improving economically when compared to people belonging to the higher castes. Interestingly, high caste people have begun to feel deprived and increasingly unhappy as soon as their reference world extended beyond the Gangetic basin and they began to compare their status with the global standard; whereas the traditionally low caste and impure people are beginning to derive much benefit out of the extended market economy where they can sell their services and products at competitive rates.

### *Fatalism and Responsibility*

The sense of responsibility is also affected by fatalism. Fatalism contributes to the development of a personality which is devoid of a sense of internalized responsibility towards society at large. Under fatalism, responsibility is continually displaced to the outside, typically to the supernatural. There is a constant external focus for the individual, as the external is the locus of power, of pleasure and prosperity, and of punishment. The individual simply does not have control. This is in sharp contrast to the Western case, and even to that of the East Asians. Westerners are highly internalized, with a strong sense of inner personal control, and their social behaviour is regulated by a similarly internalized sense of responsibility. East Asians have a stronger collective sense and external orientation, but they are also strongly internalized when it comes to social responsibility. The sense of responsibility to family, or to particular members of the family, such as the mother, and the feeling of guilt arising from the driving force behind achievement motivation.

In Nepal, people know that there is work which has to be done but they also know that this means low status. Anyone who does not have to work but can ask others to work for them is higher in status than those who work when asked by people at higher levels. Anyone who is educated, and thereby is in a position to identify with the traditional role of the high caste, would never want to work. A great majority of the educated people do not work themselves but expect that others will do what needs to be done by them. When the bulk of the educated share this perspective, little work actually gets done. Supported by this value system, people with a choice would not feel guilty for not working. Yet, ironically, the same people do not feel bad about criticizing others for not doing what they themselves would not do. This means that everybody ends up being critical of everybody else but does not necessarily feel guilty for not fulfilling his own formal duties. Lack of personal responsibility for work is excused by the belief that it is the supreme god who finishes all incompleted work in any case.

Concepts of rights, privileges and obligations, take on a special limited meaning in a hierarchic society, in that they exist only in connection with caste. One's social circumstances are basically a matter of fate. Karma denies any possibility of holding oneself responsible for one's status in society and condition in life. If people are in less privileged positions this is a matter of their fate. To interfere with their lot is to interfere with the divine order and dharmic purpose. People are in less privileged positions in order to learn critical lessons in life necessary for their spiritual advancement paralleling the caste hierarchy. From a hierarchic perspective, to make things easy and to improve their lot is to interfere in their growth and jeopardize their life-work.

Charity is not valued under Hinduism—charity being strongly distinguished from giving alms to the holy. Altruism is suspect. Similarly, one is never obliged to anyone for anything because everything occurs as it should. No sense of obligation is instilled. When a priest receives a gift, he never thanks the giver. It is the giver, the client, who should be thanking the priest for accepting it, for in accepting it the priest bestows spiritual merit on the giver. Though there are ways of expressing gratitude, 'thank you' does not exist in the Nepali vocabulary and a new word 'dhanyabad' has been coined recently as the translation of the English thanks.

*Fatalism and the Sense of Competence*

If things are fated then it becomes difficult to attribute success or failure to individual action. Personal success must always be contained within limits imposed by social expectations, and these expectations are always low. If one's life circumstances are fated, then personal success based on what is clearly individual effort and capability runs counter to these social expectations. Success due to personal competence is essentially threatening to the social order, which is cemented by rigidities ensured not only by threats of external sanction but by the lack of personal motivation for change. This lack of personal motivation is, in turn, ensured by the perception that personal effort has little effect. A demonstration of personal competence leading to success is therefore both deviant and threatening. The collective response to personal competence, then, is negative, so that the person who demonstrates competence tends inevitably to be isolated and undermined. Demonstrated personal competence leading to success is a clear rebuttal of the fatalist perspective, and fatalistic society is quick to contain and destroy it.

The current dominant value system also does not teach people to accept responsibility for their failures or to accept defeat with dignity and grace. Though it might be part of the universal human condition, with an orientation to the external, as opposed to the self, as the locus of causation, it becomes even easier to blame others or external circumstances for failure. Rarely does failure get attributed to the deity. Instead, it is deflected to the human realm. For instance, students are not ashamed of failure, for which they take no personal responsibility, but get annoyed or angry with someone else within the system, typically the teacher or the examiner. That applies equally to political workers and business people who are neither willing to take the blame nor ashamed of themselves if they fail in their own responsibilities.

*Fatalism and Complex Social Relations*

Besides a lack of achievement motivation, there are important interpersonal consequences that accrue as a result of the failure to internalize personal responsibility. A marked outcome of strongly fatalistic beliefs is that people do not feel bound to keep any form of contractual relations. From the fatalistic perspective, there is no free will or choice in decision-making, nor in how an event will unfold. Agreements can only be made subject to fate. If they are completed it is because they were fated to be completed, not because the parties to an agreement felt bound by it and were determined to see it done.

The caste system itself imposes further constraints on the ability to keep contractual relations as a result of collective pressures that compromise the ability to perform responsibly. Individuals are often subject to demands made by people of higher status than themselves. The services of the low caste will always go to meet the demands originating at the highest level. A low caste patron may make an agreement for an exchange of goods or services, but this agreement can be readily pre-empted by any later demands from someone higher up. Therefore it is a common practice for less powerful patrons not to rely on promises and pledges made by the artisan classes, such as tailors, cobblers, carpenters, masons, smiths or any such people who provide skilled or unskilled services. Low caste people have thus developed a reputation for being untrustworthy. Therefore, it has become a common belief that one has to be born high caste to be able to command respect or trust.

Besides contractual relations, the Nepali capacity for competitive behaviour is also compromised by fatalism and hierarchic factors. Many of the models used in planning the economic development of Nepal are based on cultural assumptions of economic behaviour that may have limited applicability outside of the societies for which these models were originally developed. One such set of assumptions has to do with competitive behaviour, as it is through competition that market forces are able to ensure economic efficiency. Socialist models tend to do away with competition; though this too may be a thing of the past. Fatalism also acts to hinder competition by affecting the strength of self-interested behaviour and the profit motive (which are disparaged as low caste), and strategic thought (which violates fatalistic premises). Ancient Nepali society was established and prospered through trade, so that the necessary qualities for a strong economic transformation of the country does exist but only outside the bounds of fatalism and hierarchic behaviour.

*Temporal Orientation*

Contributing to this widespread sense of fatalism is the peculiar Nepali sense of time. For Nepalis, time is like a flowing river: very few people think of discrete quantities of water in relation to the flow of river and, similarly, Nepali time is continuous without any sense of beginning or end or particular divisions. One day is just like another and one year like the previous or following one. Nepali culture does not have a sense of time as past, present and future; it is always an endless present and past is usually reckoned only in a transcendental sense. A culture which constantly harps on the theme of the spirituality and the meaninglessness of material interests reckons time in terms of this life, the life hereafter and the previous life in a cycle of ages and eons.

No Nepali child, particularly among caste people, is ever reminded of time as a commodity or a unit within which they can complete only a certain amount of work. In Nepal there is no sense of wasting time, as in other industrially advanced countries of the world. People are directly or indirectly reminded that life is a continuing present in a continuum of ages and life sequences. The future is taken seriously only in the sense of a life hereafter. People worry considerably about life after death, often to the detriment of their present circumstances. Many beautiful monuments, temples, water spouts, rest houses and rest platforms, have not been built to improve living conditions for the aged or for the sake of others but only to ensure a better life after death as a result of merit accumulated by such action. The prevalent religious faith does not encourage Nepalis to look back at the past nor does it encourage planning for the future. Within this transcendentalism the present is also unreal, transitory, mundane and a nuisance to be endured or tolerated; it is not to be taken seriously. The real world of the west is not the real world of the high caste Hindus; these are fundamentally different ontologies. Western economic development theorists and foreign aid administrators continually ignore this difference and retreat into their own ethnocentrism, which is of little help in untangling the problems of development facing Nepal.

As a rule Nepalis do not plan for the future. It is far easier to mentally speculate on the next life in an imaginary hell or heaven than to plan for one's own old age or for even later years. Peculiarities in temporal orientation, then, interact strongly with the lack of a sense of internal personal control and achievement motivation to frustrate the ability for planning which must surely have important consequences on Nepal's ability to navigate the future.

Traditionally, the more free time a person has the higher and more important he is considered to be. A busy person is usually running errands for someone higher up, so he can not be of high caste or high status himself.

The Nepali sense of history has become distorted as well, and it is important to note this distortion as it perpetuates the separation of Nepali mentality from the world's view of what is real. There was no interest in historical studies until a few decades ago. The *Puranas* were confused with history, and it is still so today, and pundits, replete with the knowledge of the *Puranas*, keep confusing mythical personalities with historic ones and ancient Indian cultural history with that of Nepal. Future life was, and is, imagined on the basis of an imaginary unreal past life rather than on projections and planning grounded in a careful study of yesteryears; i.e., myth substitutes history and mystical images of the future substitute the need for concrete planning.

These peculiarities in the Nepali sense of time have implications in many areas of social, collective and individual life. Most people live in the present and are principally consummatory in their orientation, rather than instrumental. They squander whatever food, grain, or money they get at once without any consideration for the future. Consequently, they suffer from unnecessary deprivation due to their lack of planning for the future and due to the mismanagement of resources under their control. Being highly consummatory, no savings take place and there can be no investment. The society must remain dependent on foreign investment in the future, not simply because of the low economic level of development, but largely because of a constitutional cultural predisposition towards present consumption.

There is an awareness that this Nepali sense of time is not shared by other cultures. Some Nepalis have a habit of making a clear distinction between traditional attitudes towards time and punctuality. Such people would even go so far as to identify the differences by using identifiers such as 'English time' and 'Nepali time'. Whenever appointments are made, they would be confirmed by asking 'Nepali time or English time?' By 'English time' they mean the exact and punctual hour of the appointment, but 'Nepali time' infers a casual appointment, later than the time mentioned by at least an hour or two and sometimes not taking place at all. The use of the expression 'English time' is fading since the English presence is no longer so strong after they left the subcontinent; and many other western people of various nationalities have been visiting and working in Nepal in different capacities and at different levels. Among these western people are many who do not insist upon or even expect punctuality. They are researchers, university students, volunteers, tourists, hippies, individual trekkers and a variety of others. None of them impose their sense of time on the Nepalis they come in contact with, so the 'English time' concept of punctuality is fading.

There are exceptions now, and many people are punctual for appointments if they believe that the meeting is a significant one and of direct benefit to themselves.

However, most people are still totally unaware of the damage they do to their own future by being casual in their attitude towards time resource and are not able to see the bad effect they might be causing by being an hour late for an appointment. They are insensitive to the inconvenience they cause other people. Again the situation is complicated by factors arising from peculiarities in the status system. Hierarchy dictates that the person who is to be visited is ranked higher than the visitor. It is acceptable, for the most part, to be late. The latecomer knows that all he has to do is to apologize and he will be pardoned; forgiving behaviour is considered to be high caste.

Nepali society considers time as non-essential with no importance of its own. The difference between timely action and belated action has no meaning. People are forced to undertake actions quite unwillingly, and only when they have no alternative or escape. This results in either no action, belated action, or sloppy action, all of which combine to keep production at a minimum and the economy impoverished. The whole national culture, based on fatalistic values, manages to do everything at the eleventh hour. It can only be hoped that this culture of timelessness will be replaced, though pundits insist that the concept of timelessness is the hallmark of Hindu civilization.

### *Fatalism and Authority*

Within the hierarchic worldview, the caste system is a direct manifestation of an essential and natural social order. It is the embodiment of an absolute truth, decreed and protected by deity. There is no doubt of its legitimacy, either with regard to its overall general or to its particular concrete form. Consequently, it is inflexible and intolerant of experimentation and change. Authority is derived from spiritual necessity and from deity, and is bestowed and ultimately administered by the priests. The primary preoccupation of the Bahuns is supposed to be with spiritual matters; the agency of the fates or deity in the regulation of society is passed to the Thakuri-Chhetris, who rule essentially by divine right. The Guptas of the Licchavi period went so far as to proclaim the Gupta ruler a living manifestation of Vishnu.

Outside of religious texts prescribing caste-related social behaviour there has been little formal legal development in Nepali society. As considered above in discussing responsibility, social regulation is not well internalized in a caste society, and is largely the consequence of developed passivity and a lack of motivation for change. Active regulation is secondary to passive acquiescence, and must thus be located externally to the individual, in socially applied sanctions. As considered in the chapters on caste and socialization, the agencies for such external sanctioning, the caste and village councils and family, are not overly developed for this particular function, and there are few rules or laws that exist to be broken. Punishment is rare, and tends to be in the form of social exclusion.Therefore people at higher social or political levels can violate laws and commit offences with impunity.

*Dependency*

In the Nepali context, instrumental action mostly takes place within a system of dominant-submissive relations where the dominant force is located primarily at a supernatural level, though certain segments of society do directly benefit as the mediators of such a relationship, i.e., the priests. They may take advantage of their position, but essentially they are not an actively exploiting class. They are victims of the system, as well as benefactors, and their benefits have not translated into excessive material advantage, for their purpose is ultimately of a spiritual kind. The priests themselves are not in control of their circumstances and are, like the other castes, equally subjected to determined fate.

The submissive character of the Nepali may well be a manifestation of a more basic disposition towards dependency. In cross-cultural research, contrasts in the degree to which a culture modally tends towards independence and dependence have been made and found to be useful. A study of dependency in Nepal also would seem to be important, and in particular there is a developed form of dependency that is very characteristic of Nepali society, an understanding of which is essential to an appreciation of Nepali social interaction.

In the previous chapter I described something of the pattern of socialization within Nepal, and the factors responsible for developing dependency. Late weaning, lack of toilet training, casual parental use of punishment, close supervision at early ages along with the general indulgence in the young all contribute to high dependence. There is no shocking immersion into an adult world of extreme and weighty responsibility, as is found in East Asia; there is no training for independence, as is found in the West; there is nothing to really mark the end of childhood and the commencement of adulthood. Social responsibilities, especially to aid the family in its subsistent economic solvency by tending sheep and goats, are assumed early but do not represent a severe disjuncture from previous life. Such work responsibilities are heavily intermingled with play. Dependency is highly characteristic of the Nepali, but can be distinguished from dependency in other cultures, for instance, in the Japanese society, where dependence is more upon the mother (Doi,1962,1971) unlike Nepal where it is more on the father.

Dependency can have positive as well as negative consequences. Positively, it may be a factor supporting harmonious cooperative action—a hallmark of ethnic village society. Dependency on others and the ready ability to form substitute father figures is also one of the reasons that makes it easier for the Nepalis to adapt to strange situations. Whenever Nepalis receive good treatment from anyone and feel comfortable they begin to identify that individual with a father figure. Some western people find it awkward when their domestic staff or subordinates announce that 'you are like a father to me'. Or perhaps worse, they do not understand what is implied by the comment. Being placed in the role of the father figure, the father-surrogate is expected to provide the nurturance of a father, including physical sustenance and general concern for the welfare of that individual. The dependent character, once embedded in this new quasi- paternal relationship is again complete and secure.

In the caste society, the dependent relationship is not a horizontal one, between peers with specialized resources which in exchange become the basis of the social fabric. Society here is not based on interdependency, as it is among various ethnic communities, in the West and increasingly in East Asia. Instead, society is based very much on systems of vertical dependency which parallels the caste system but is also somewhat separate from it. This paternal dependency may well exist independently of caste. Nepali society emphasizes a continuing superordinate and subordinate relationship between father and son on the one hand, and mother and daughter on the other. The potential for father substitution then extends vertically dependent relationships out of the family and into the mainstream of society. In Nepal, this relationship outside of the family has been institutionalized, and is called *chakari*.

## *Chakari*

Within Hinduism, chakari is an essential concept which means to wait upon, to serve, to appease, or to seek favour from a god. When someone goes to a temple and makes an offering or prays to the deity, they are performing chakari. Chakari was officially introduced into secular life during the Rana period, mainly as a form of control designed to keep potential rivals or opponents away from belligerent activities. These potential rivals were required to spend time generally in attendance at the Rana palaces, where at certain hours the Ranas would be able to observe them physically and know that they were not somewhere else fomenting trouble. This was done very formally, usually in the afternoon, and the hours set aside for this purpose were known as the chakari hours.

With time the practice of chakari was recognized as a criterion for judging loyalty and reliability, and was applid even to less privileged kinsmen as well as other Nepali officials. Anyone who did not appear for chakari was immediately suspected as at least unreliable and therefore unworthy of retaining a job. Promotion for such people was out of the question. Consequently, government employees had to perform chakari to ensure job security and in order to be eligible for promotion. Actual job performance was not of paramount importance, although sometimes it could be an added criterion for promotion. Those seeking improvement in life via this practice are called chakariwal, people practising chakari (Bista 1989b).

With the end of the Ranas, chakari was formally abolished, but by then it had firmly installed itself as an integral feature of Nepali social organization. Though it will be commonly denied, today chakari remains an important part of social life, and is evident at all levels of government. Typically, chakari is performed in the morning and at the house of the person whose favours are being cultivated, when there is some assurance of actually seeing him. Some chakariwal go into the house and remain there for several hours, mostly in the courtyard, do their greetings and then leave. Others perform chakari every other day or irregularly. Besides presenting oneself and offering greetings, other forms of chakari include offering gifts, either material gifts or gifts in services and favours. For the important, there will be a number of chakariwal in attendance everyday.

The form of the chakari will vary with the status differential between the chakariwal and the person to whom chakari is being offered. With high status differential, the chakariwal is particularly obeisant and is more likely to offer various services. As the differential decreases the obeisance turns into a simple greeting, and gifts are more likely to substitute for services. Eventually, when the status differential is bridged, chakari is transformed into another Nepali institution, called afno manchhe, which will be considered shortly.

One of the main kinds of services performed in chakari is the transference of information. This information might be meant to amuse the patron, benefit him, or consist simply of things that he would like to hear,particularly about rivals.[1] It is in the transfer of information that chakari has assumed particular importance, and there it has even developed certain very positive characteristics. The chakari system has to a large extent become coextensive with the informal structuring of Nepali organizations — it is a way for information to be passed throughout the organization outside formal channels. Through it the person higher up in the organizational hierarchy is able to obtain extensive information about operations at all levels of the organization, and hence it has the potential to become a valuable tool for effective management. Chakari also has a therapeutic function and helps equalize ralations, providing opportunities for those at lower levels of the hierarchy to express their ideas and air their grievances. Most grievance procedures are effected through chakari channels. Once the chakariwal becomes a source of beneficial information then a reverse dependency is developed on the chakariwal, and this can lead to an equalization of status.

Chakari is a public event, open to the view of all. This is important as it minimizes accusations of conspiracy. Once the substance of the relationship is based on information exchange it is only possible to become a chakariwal to a single patron. One cannot be a chakariwal to a number of people because then he cannot be considered to be trustworthy, especially if the various patrons are rivals and in competition.

The gift donor in chakari has certain rights. There is an obligation on the part of the recipient to respond to the chakariwal when the chakariwal so determines. It is possible at that point to hedge the obligation but this is difficult and must be done with an explanation (example 'I can't offer you this job because of other pressing concerns but I can offer you something else either now or in the future.') Ultimately there has to be a balance in exchange relations.

Further, there is a general obligation to accept the first gift from the chakariwal, as chakari is seen as an integral part of social organization, and to refuse chakari is to disrupt the social organization. As just mentioned, chakari plays a critical role in the informal operations of Nepali organizational life, and to reject it is often taken as a sign of bad or compromised management. When a young idealist, fresh from training in the west, attempts to operate without chakari, this can be regarded as offensive to subordinates, who now no longer have this critical informal avenue for grievance procedures open to them, and to their superiors, who then regard them as disruptive and out of touch with their work environment. Chakari is so ingrained in Nepali organizational life that to persist in attempting to exclude it is seen to be deviant — a demonstration of arrogance and conceit by those above and below.

The recipient of chakari has some informal rights of discrimination, but only within limits. Chakari is very public, theoretically open to all, all castes, but effectively not so accessible. If the chakariwal is seen to have some functional relevance to the operations of the social organization, then that chakariwal would have to be accepted. But for a stranger, someone with no clear connection to the relevant social organizations for which the patron owned some responsibility, these rights do not at first exist and must be demonstrated. A Limbu from Limbuwan, for example, with an insignificant gift, would have to compete against an established chakariwal and it would be easier for the patron to reject the gift and the chakariwal. The chakariwal has to be noticed by the patron in order to be heard, so that with many chakariwals it is easy to ignore particular individuals. A lot depends again on status differential and other factors, such as the quality of the gift, the kind of chakariwal and his appearance, and so on. The only option for such a stranger who desires to become a chakariwal is to persist in his attendance until he is finally noticed. Except in this extreme kind of case chakariwal has to be accepted.

Sometimes chakari takes the form of a bribe or other form of corruption. Caplan's account of one of the district headquarters of an outlying area reveals this aspect quite clearly:

> A few of the wealthiest men in the district today owe their wealth entirely to their careers in local administration and most government employees who spent long years in their posts were able to purchase lands, however menial their work, and negligible their salaries...some senior officials are said never to have accepted cash, while others acquired reputations for extreme rapaciousness (Caplan, 1971:273).

Further Caplan's informants told him that,

> The practice of Chakari is considered a necessary and appropriate method of getting employment...It is recognized as demeaning to the supplicant, but no man loses esteem in the eyes of other residents if he demonstrates weakness before and dependence upon the administration. To do this is merely to accept reality. (ibid., 274).

Within a system characterized by parental dependency, people in exalted positions (the father-surrogates) consider giving favours to those who demonstrate dependence on them through chakari as normal and proper behaviour. It is gratifying and flattering to them to be able to do so. But gradually they fall prey to the inherent vices of chakari. Once a gift is accepted the obligation of the patron to respond to the chakariwal, typically on the chakariwal's terms, is also established. As the gifts increase, the size of the social debt increases and the patron effectively looses control of the relationship. This readily leads to a point where the patron is forced into actions that he would not normally perform, and that are not in the best interests of his higher obligations to the organization of which he is a part. The more strategically placed in society the patron is, the greater the ramifications. Decisions are made, appointments determined because of pressing obligations formed through chakari and not as a result of an objective determination of what is best at the point. The entire social apparatus then suffers as critical positions are filled and governmental decisions made as a result of chakari. It is a built-in guarantor of incompetence, inefficiency, and misplaced effort.

While there are some positive aspects in the chakari system, on the whole chakari plays a negative role in the administrative and political life. The root of this lies in a deep-seated paranoia that is evident in politics and bureaucracy, the fear that someone out there is doing something adverse to one's own well being, particularly in using the chakari system of information transfer to plant rumours and lies. As considered above, under fatalism there is no belief in genuine personal control over one's future, and certain elements have to be constantly appeased, either powerful supernatural elements or other powerful administrative ones. If things do not progress smoothly or, worse, things start to happen unfavourably, then the tendency is to blame the deceitful actions of others. These others can be at any level of the organization; in a horizontal relation to the paranoic, or vertically subordinate or superordinate. The remedy is counter-action; using the same chakari system to undermine the credibility of one's imagined opponents by spreading gossip and fabrications against them. If the imagined enemy is at a superordinate level, chakari allows one to bypass that level and appeal to an even more senior level. Consequently, no one is safe from these self-perpetuating paranoid machinations. The situation becomes archetypal of the classical intrigue, the bane of many former societies. Such intrigue tends to be characteristic of the downward phase of a society; not a prelude to its efflorescence. Nepali society cannot develop as long as chakari characterizes its organizational life.

During the Rana days people bragged about their being a 'chakariwal', say of a certain Shamsher Jung Bahadur Rana. Today's Nepal has officially adopted democracy. Therefore people do not brag about being a 'chakariwal' but those who have ambition and are interested in self-promotion know that this cannot be achieved without chakari. The hierarchic attitude of the people encourages chakari in two ways: first, it is considered important to reach ever higher levels in the hierarchy, which cannot be achieved without chakari; secondly, once one believes in the hierarchic order of things, it is not considered lowering of one's position to be servile to individuals who stand on the higher rungs of the social or political ladder.

*Individualism and Social Relations*

As seen in the earlier discussion on kinship, class, and caste groups, most Nepalis are embedded within a complex social structure. To a large extent, their self identity is determined by the social roles they assume as members of such groups, and their social orientation might be defined as traditionally being group-oriented or collectivistic. This traditional group orientation is being gradually replaced by the development of an individualistic orientation, a development which is being made at the cost of a community and national consciousness.

The individualism developing among the younger generations in Nepal is not yet a mature one as is found, perhaps, in the west, but has a strong element of egotism. More than a hundred years ago Alexis de Tocqueville commented :

> Individualism is a novel expression to which a novel ideal has given birth. Our fathers were only acquainted with egotism. Egotism is a passionate and exaggerated love of self, which leads a man to connect everything with his own person, and to prefer himself to everything in the world. Individualism is a mature and calm feeling, which disposed each member of the community to sever himself from the mass of his fellow creatures; and to draw apart from his family and his friends; so that after he has thus formed a little circle of his own, he willingly leaves society at large to itself.(Tocqueville, 1954,reprint).

Nepali individualism operates largely at the more primitive egotistic stage. To some extent this is a conscequence of the preoccupation with maintaining caste purity. The upper caste people think in terms of one's individual position vis-a-vis the Matwali people. They have to keep in mind constantly a number of things when going outside the home. They have to take care of the food they eat, who cooks it and what kind of food it is. They have to be concerned with who they touch or are in close proximity with. This keeps them constantly on guard, while forcing a certain ego-focus.

In the last chapter reference was made to other factors which contribute to a sense of social estrangement among high caste families. Bahuns are by birth at the higher levels of spiritual purity, but this is a purity that others can easily contaminate. At an early age children in such families are taught that they are different from others and must keep their distance from them because they are defiling. They grow up being unable to play with other children and do not lead the lifestyle of other children. In many areas of Nepal, they live on the periphery of society, descended from immigrant families that are forced to move in every generation in order to find new religious clients. Because the caste system has never really become established in Nepal outside of the Kathmandu Valley, their dependence on caste has ensured that they remain disembodied from the real social fabric of the country.

Priests find it very difficult to develop close relations and a working respect for others, qualities necessary for effective social relations. Their interpersonal relationships are not of the same quality as that of other castes, and this is apparent to other Nepalis who deal with them. They operate much more from a position of enforced individualism. They find it difficult to develop a sense of the other, since the other is inherently different and strange. Such people can be good rhetoricians on the general welfare of society but find it impossible to work concretely with a group to help others. This robs them of gentleness and kindness to others, as well as a sense of humour.

This is not at all true of the non-caste ethnic people. They have grown up as a part of society and their positions are not dependent on caste purity but have other strong social and political antecedents. It does not particularly matter to them if they touch and are touched by others. They can be developed to a stage of full reciprocity with others. And the others respond to this. In bureaucratic relations, also, it is an ethnic individual who can work cooperatively and emphathically. The high caste individual uses a different style, focusing on erudition and punditry. With the prevalent system of education and the principles of recruitment at the civil service, it is the high caste people who are becoming more prevalent in the administrative bureaucracy and not the ethnic group member. This has severe implications for the efficiency of administration.

Very few people treat high positions with responsibility, as a duty to society at large. Many see a high position as a reward, something to be enjoyed. In contrast, individuals from ethnic groups act cooperatively and are not socially or psychologically isolated from their fellow citizens. This has been described in several ethnographic studies conducted among many ethnic groups in Nepal. There would be no one to help cultivate or plough their land or give support to them during house-building if they did not have mutual respect and trust in their fellow villagers. The same attitude, when applied in administrative offices, tend to make the higher officers of ethnic background more successful in achieving the goals set for them.

*Group Behaviour and Afno Manchhe*

There are very few Nepalis who are willing to leave their own secure inner circle, let alone be an individualist in Tocqueville's sense. When we consider the sense of belonging which an individual requires in order to feel safe and secure, we also include the logical consequence of this need to constantly maintain one's own inner circle. Nepalis make a strong distinction between us and them. People who do not belong to one's own inner circle are perceived as being non-persons and there is no real concern over what happens to such unrelated individuals. Time and effort is exhausted in taking care of one's own people so that there is little energy or inclination left to be concerned about non-persons.

The distinction between the group 'us' and the rest as 'them' manifests itself in every walk of social, cultural, political and economic life. Everything inside the circle of 'us' is predictable and the rest is external and unpredictable. Therefore, there is a constant need to maintain the boundary. The maintenance of the inner groups is achieved in a number of ways. Gathering people together for ritualistic festive occasions is one. In rural areas, among the various people funeral rites, anniversaries, and feasts are the main occasions which help foster the sense of solidarity with the inner group, while, recently, in urban areas, invitations to wedding feasts and the distribution of greeting cards during the Dasain festival and the Nepali New Year are newly found occasions on which to define the consistency of one's own circle. In recent years even some foreigners such as volunteers, university and college students living with Nepali families have been included by Nepalis within their circle of afno manchhe. They receive intimate and close behaviour which a career professional working at official and formal level would never receive.

Afno manchhe is the term used to designate one's inner circle of associates — it means 'one's own people' and refers to those who can be approached whenever need arises. The strength or weakness of anyone is measured in terms of the quality and quantity of the circles of afno manchhe he is a part of. Afno manchhe is a critical Nepali institution. It is integrally connected with the smooth functioning of society. For example, a bank teller takes longer to cash a cheque if the customer is a 'non-person' but makes a special effort if the customer is a member of his circle and therefore afno manchhe. The reputation of the bank becomes of secondary importance as the maintenance of the fence around one's own circle is primary. The same thing is true in all government and corporation offices.

The persistence of ethnic or regional identity is a manifestation of the need to have one's own circle clearly defined and maintained permanently. By inference, ethnic, regional or cultural identity would collapse only when new circles of class, profession or residential areas are created.

Within Nepal there is no point in arguing that one set of afno manchhe circles is better or worse than another. The only accountable quality in an individual is the need for membership of the circle in question. Academic qualification, training, background, working discipline, integrity of character and other such attributes are not as important or helpful as the sense of belonging to a particular circle. Many an executive tends to recognize his subordinates on the basis of membership of a circle rather than on the basis of personal qualifications, skills or other attributes of capability. A member of one's own circle is naturally preferred, even without a particular capacity to perform in some organizational role. The most important asset for anyone is not what you know, but who you know.

In Nepal, the people who display distinctly different behaviour towards a person or a non-person are usually those who have many elaborate ways and means of defining such circles. Compared to other people in Nepal, the Newars of Kathmandu show this most markedly as they have many circles and each individual belongs to several at one and the same time. These circles are defined by locale, by caste, by profession, by Guthi guild membership (and the latter include the Rotary Club, Lion's Club, Leo's Club, Reyukai, and so on). This is natural for a community which has been living in a compact urban setting for more than fifteen hundred years. Most individuals within the community have little interest in non-persons because there are too many of them as far as they are concerned. Buddhist Newars tend to have even more of such obligations reserved exclusively for their people than Hindu Shresthas who have recently come out of their defined traditional circles and have been stretching their boundaries to include other non-persons inside them, thus converting them to the status of an afno manchhe.

Nepalis will never be willing to knock down existing circles of identity unless they have the option of crossing the line from one circle to another, and this will not be possible for the vast majority of the people except for those in the middle classes in urban areas with a modern education. Nepal is too strong an ascriptive rather than an achievement oriented society to allow much mobility. But the determination of membership in a particular circle is not the simple outcome of caste or ethnicity. Caste relates to a more formal structure, and while it is still important in imposing restrictions on social movement, such restrictions are not the same as one finds, for example, in parts of the Gangetic basin. To some extent this is because Nepali caste only seems to adopt the nature of a class structure rather than being a pure caste structure. Of most importance is the fact that, except for the Bahuns, pollution is not attached to caste in the way it is in India and there is a degree of personal interaction among the castes that would never be tolerated where pollution is an important factor.

In some circumstances, untouchables act in the capacity of temple priests. Caste, then, is not an absolute barrier to inclusion or exclusion in the more informal interpersonal circles or groups being considered here. If we look carefully into the past, we find many instances where people have moved out of one circle of reference and entered another through migration, social mobility or political achievement. This has been possible in the urban areas where there are opportunities to be availed (Rosser, 1966: 90-104). One constantly tries to stretch one's own circle to make a bigger ring and include more potential resources inside it. The increasing practice of inviting individuals to social occasions such as dinners or picnic parties or to weddings, is becoming an accepted norm for enticing someone into entering a circle for the first time. This is largely practised in the urban areas among modern educated people.

## NOTES AND REFERENCES

1. In Nepal this is usually known as arkako kura launụ, or chukli launu.

CHAPTER FIVE

# POLITICS AND GOVERNMENT

After the unification of Nepal in the eighteenth century, the concern of the government was with consolidating its rule and with battling against rebellious groups. With this emphasis on control, its form was largely military. The Sugauli Treaty of 1816, which fixed the political boundaries of the nation, helped provide the sense of security that allowed the government to be less preoccupied with military affairs and to turn to other things. Much of the effort of the ruling class turned towards the cultivation of personal ambition, as the nobles and courtiers embarked on a regime of intrigue; a practice prevalent in Kathmandu through the later part of the preceding Malla period. The winner of these intra-palace machinations was Jung Bahadur Rana, who came to power in 1847 with the ill-famed Kot Massacre, when all his potential rivals were eliminated.

The King had the formal title of Shri Panch Maharajadhiraj, and within the status hierarchy continued through the Rana period in this position, though divorced from any real power. The Ranas developed another position of Shri Teen Maharaja, which was the real centre of power. This position of the Ranas has been interpreted as that of Prime Minister, though, in more strict terms, it is really a graded rank of kingship. Jung Bahadur was given the title of the Maharaja of Kaski and Lamjung principalities, which were independent prior to their being integrated under the unified kingdom of Nepal in the eighteenth century. The Ranas, then, were kings in their own right, though of a less formal rank than the Shahs. The family rule of the Ranas continued for over a hundred years, from 1847 to 1950.

The orientation of the Ranas was towards furthering the fortunes of their family, not of the country, and patriotism was even regarded suspiciously as a threat to their personal interests. Thus, the Ranas had a strong personal motivation in their work, combined with effective control over their administrative resources, which were discreet and manageable. In furthering their family interests, the Ranas were able administrators, and there remains, in some quarters, a nostalgic regard for their apparent competence. The certainty of their authority had much to do with their effectiveness, and the methods for gaining access to this authority were clearly established, operating with the assistance of afno manchhe and chakari.

Rivals within the Rana family were controlled by their de facto banishment to the provinces under the guise of being awarded governorships. Non-Rana rivals had to be handled in other ways, especially because their potential power bases existed in these provincial areas. It was to control these non-Rana rivals as well as the disgruntled junior Ranas, that the chakari system was developed and formalized. Suspect nobles were required to be in close proximity to the Ranas, and to formally and publicly attend the Ranas at certain predetermined hours each day. By being restrained in this manner, and restricted from travelling anywhere outside of Kathmandu, these rivals would not be able to build up their power bases elsewhere in the country. Visiting each other at night within Kathmandu was made impossible by the imposition of a curfew. The practice of chakari was adopted with a different intent. It signified both respect and a willingness to be seen as personally committed to the chakari patron, and was used at all levels of the Rana administration.

Although, the Rana rule was primarily a family-run business, with little interest in the welfare of the country, there were exceptions. After the First World War, the Rana Prime Minister, Shri Maharaja Chandra Shamsher, introduced the first real attempts at modernization: a college, a small railroad near the Indian border, a hydroelectric power plant in Kathmandu Valley, a few miles of roads, hospitals in several parts of the country, and the first street lighting in Kathmandu. Later, taking the cue from the shortage of supplies during the Second World War, Juddha Shamsher established several factories for the production of basic consumer goods in eastern Terai. With the end of the war and the recuperation of traditional supplies elsewhere, prices dropped and the infant industries of the Terai quickly folded. Thus, at the time of the Rana overthrow, Nepal was still in many ways a medieval oriental state.

A change occurred during the reign of the late king, Tribhuvan. Encouraged by Indian Independence and the sense of change experienced everywhere, especially in the third-world countries, authority was placed in the hands of the people most active in the campaign against the Ranas. They operated with the active encouragement and indirect participation of the new Indian Government. Several dozen political parties were formed, representing views from the extreme left to the extreme right. These parties were essentially lobbying bodies. A parliament was formed, with members nominated by the King upon recommendation of the political parties, but it was only an advisory body to the King and the Cabinet. Real power resided with the Cabinet and the Ministries, and the civil service bureaucracy, the model for which was imported from India.

This system was not inherently stable, with the various opposition parties provoking factional strife which led to mass demonstrations and strikes. Fatalistic values also compromised the possibility of an effective political system, whose primary aim was to elevate the quality of life in the country to modern standards. People had yet to learn that things do not come by god's design even though the teachings of the pundits continued to tell them that they do. While the desire for the material benefits of modernism was increasing, there was no corresponding increase in strategic activity to realize these desires. By 1958, the system had been enervated.

In 1959, a general election was held to create a democratic parliament. The election was won by the Nepali Congress Party (NCP), who had over seventy per cent of the votes and consequently formed the Cabinet. There was an immediate reaction to this. Many felt that the NCP was not acting in the interests of the country. There was widespread unrest in different parts of the country against the NCP and, consequently, against the government.

In 1960, the late King Mahendra, who remained at all times the ultimate power in Nepal, decided that this party system was not going to work and was not the appropriate instrument to facilitate rapid development. He declared all parties illegal, closed down the parliament, arrested and imprisoned all cabinet members then in Kathmandu, and took the government into his own hands. An advisory council was formed, primarily with defectors from the NCP, which then acted as a Cabinet. The constitution was amended in 1962 and the first National Panchayat formed, with representatives elected from districts. The election did not involve a universal franchise but was restricted to individuals invited by District Governors, who voted by a show of hands. The National Panchayat, at this stage, was mainly an advisory body. The King continued to nominate his own Cabinet Ministers. In the late sixties, the King again created the position of Prime Minister as chairman of the Cabinet, with other appointments rotating, in response to political exigencies in the country. Throughout, the civil services remained intact and effectively ran the country. In 1980 there was a referendum to determine whether the Nepali government should operate with a partyless Panchayat System with appropriate reforms or a multiparty system. As a result of the referendum, the partyless system was endorsed, primarily as a means of avoiding institutionalized factionalism and the inter-party hostility. A new constitution was drafted to facilitate the smooth working of the partyless political system.

Under this third ammended constitution, the ultimate power of government resided with the King. The constitution provided adult franchise for general elections to the Rasthriya Panchayat (National Assembly), the supreme legislative body of the country, every five years. Hundred and twelve representatives were elected from seventy-five districts, and a maximum of eighteen were nominated from among the academicians, representatives of special class organizations (youth, ex-military, adult, women, peasants, labour), and from among ethnic minorities. The class organizations were a special feature. Because there was no party system, these groups were meant to look after the interests of their members. Membership in any class group was exclusive of membership in any other, with the youth group representing all those between twenty to forty. The officials of these organizations were elected by their members, and these elections were at times more intense than the Panchayat elections, in part because the electorate for the class organizations was nation-wide and not local.

The Prime Minister was elected by a two-third majority in the National Panchayat and, once he was approved by the King, he formed the Cabinet from members of the National Panchayat, which remained, in principle, directly responsible to the National Panchayat. However in reality this principle as embodied in the constitution was frequently ignored to suit the interests of the people in power. By 1988 it was clear that the people with strong authoritarian tendencies were beginning to strangle the democratic process of the Panchayat System (see Bista 1989a). This antagonised even the people within the Panchayat system who supported the liberal democratic process. Consequently, the people, under the leadership of the Nepali Congress and the United Front of the various factions of the Communist Party rebelled against the Partyless Panchayat System which collapsed under the pressure of a very strong popular uprising in April 1990.

The country under the Panchayat regime was divided into five development zones for purposes of planning and the execution of development projects. The entire country was also divided into fourteen political zones (anchal), headed by fourteen commissioners, nominated by the King. The Zonal Commissioners (Anchaladhis) were responsible primarily for political activities, including the maintenance of law and order and overall responsibility for the development of the zone. They maintained the liaison between local government bodies and the national government. This practice has been discontinued and the Zonal Commissioners' positions have been dissolved since May 1990.

The country is also divided into a total of seventy-five administrative districts, each headed by a Chief District Officer, a regular civil servant. The districts are responsible for the building and maintenance of such things as roads and bridges and for distribution of government grants to the different villages. Each district administration consists of branch offices of the ministries of local development, transportation, communications, education, forestry, agriculture, water resources, finance, industry, commerce, and some other departments. Technical ministries are represented by technical personnel, such as engineers, agricultural experts and medical people. The District Secretariat comprises all the ministry officials at the district level and the various offices of civil engineers, health assistants, and other professional government employees necessary for the running of district operations.

Below the district level, each of the seventy five districts has a number of Village Panchayats, which are formed on the basis of population. Village populations averaging between three thousand and five thousand warrant the creation of a Village Panchayat. In addition to this, there are thirty-three towns: the biggest being that of Kathmandu. Some of the bigger towns have municipalities which take care of the development and maintenance of public facilities, such as local roads, temples, the local water supply, public buildings, urban development, education and collection of taxes.

There is a Supreme Court with judges appointed by the King, and there are also Zonal Courts in all fourteen zones and District Courts in all seventy-five districts. Village councils are authorized to act as courts of justice on disputes of a local nature and petty feuds, except for criminal cases. Until 1963, the law decreed differential punishment for different castes, by gender, and for people of different socio-political backgrounds. But today, everyone is equal in the eyes of the law.

This complex administrative structure has developed only during the past couple of decades, specifically to aid development and for the modernization of the country. An administrative machinery of this size requires vast resources for its maintenance. The investment of resources in the development of such a large bureaucratic apparatus significantly preceded the development of the technical-economic infrastructure that was really needed for genuine development, and the contribution of such an apparatus to real development has been negligible. The government has developed a certain kind of organicity so that it has a life of its own, is self perpetuating, with its internal dynamism largely insensitive to its external environment and the functions that it should be fulfilling for the society at large. Most things get done by default, or by processes where strategic planning and coordinated action play little part.

Overseeing the general development of the country is the National Planning Commission (NPC), whose purpose is to develop the five year plans that would methodically and efficiently modernize the country, bringing its standard of living up to that of developed Asian countries by the turn of the century. The NPC is directly under the Prime Minister, as its chairman, and its five or six members, mostly economists, statisticians, and geographers, are sworn in by the King upon the recommendation of the Prime Minister. In practice, the five-year plan document is worth very little. Roads and schools do get built, but most often in areas not designated by the NPC. They are not constructed in consultation with the representatives of foreign aid organizations, who provide many of the resources to be used, and this leads to disparities in the perceived priorities of development between the foreign aid donors and the NPC. The NPC also tends to ignore the people, local institutions, and even the Ministries once they have made their initial recommendations. Issues and disagreements are aired only at the end of planning and there is no continuing dialogue between the interested parties in the stages preceding planning.

The plan is a legally binding directive which obliges the designated ministries to put it into effect. But failure to implement the plan is excused with the argument that the NPC is insensitive to real needs or geographic circumstances that qualify the plausibility of many projects. A National Development Council was introduced by the king to air disputes on planning and with the purpose of making efforts at conciliation. But it became merely an exercise in self-aggrandizement before the King and used as an opportunity to demonstrate personal worth with the hope of administrative advancement.

To better understand how policy is actually formulated and development projects are undertaken I will give a brief overview of one particular developmental concern, the building of roads.

Road construction is the responsibility of the Roads and Transportation Ministry, which divides this task into district level activities (for local roads) and national level activities (for highways). Typically, the Ministry makes a simple determination that so many miles of roads will be built at the national level and so many at the local level. National level roads usually have to be built with foreign resources. Often the foreign aid groups have different and more economically realistic perspectives on what roads should be built and where. Consequently, for most of the national roads, except the East-West Highway, priorities are set by foreign aid considerations. Political considerations have also played an important role. The People's Republic of China, for example, has, in the past, provided funds and engineering expertise for the construction of national roads, which has been opposed by the Indian Government on the grounds that such roads would merely provide easier access for Chinese armies in any invasion of India. Chinese aid has had to be redirected, then, to accommodate Indian fears. India has also provided funds and expertise for the construction of other roads close to her border.

Local (district) roads were built on local initiative, usually as a result of district and village level decisions, in consultation with the national level representative of the area until the beginning of 1990 when the National Panchayat was dissolved. Villages were previously connected by a system of walking trails and, usually, well used trails were transformed into roads. The primary motivation was that of facilitating the transportation of goods. Some roads could be built with no outside assistance, through the cooperative action of members of the affected villages. But some roads required resources beyond those available to villages. Bridges require exotic materials (cement, iron), and engineering skills. Paving is expensive. Getting the required resources is a matter of aggressiveness and persistence. If there is an afno manchhe engineer and resources at the district level, these are used. If afno manchhe can not solve the problem, the village and district representatives approach the Ministry at one or two levels, depending upon who they are and who they have access to. The first level is that of engineers, who operate essentially at the district level. But the districts have small funds to disperse and often cannot be accommodating to such requests. Then the heads of the departments are approached, usually called

Chief Engineers. If the Chief Engineer is not forthcoming, then the Secretary of Roads and Transportation or the Minister is approached, and both afno manchhe and chakari are used. In submitting their request, the local authorities are obliged to guarantee that the unskilled labour will be provided locally.

Roads most often do get built regardless of whether they are included in the NPC plan or have been thought of after the plan has been formulated. If the petition is submitted after the formulation of a plan, work will begin and may be completed; still, the Secretary submits the petition for such roads for consideration in the next plan. The initiative for the making of roads, the lobbying for resources, and the close surveillance of the operation until it is complete, are all undertaken at the local level, and by agencies outside the Ministry.

*The Ministry Bureaucracies*

There was a bureaucracy in the Rana period but it was inconsequential to the one developed in the post-Rana period based on the Indian model. It absorbed most of the Rana administration, except for the highest Rana officials. The early administrators of the post-Rana period emulated the practices of the Rana administration. The decision making powers were concentrated in a few, and afno machhe and chakari were still the established ways of doing things. The presence of chakariwals was one of the ways of making authority evident for the new administrators and chakari became institutionalized as an integral aspect of all ministries.

Meanwhile, new patterns of bureaucratic behaviour were imported and ritualized. In order to justify the new positions bureaucratic activities were created. For those responsibile for planning, the most popular of these new self-justifying activities was the 'meeting.' These meetings and 'conferences' built up the formal atmosphere for continuous debate and speculation, and the stage for self-aggrandizement. Punditry was thereby readily accommodated within the modern bureaucratic apparatus. But punditry is an exercise of the mind and has little to do with strategic planning and the transformation of plans into actualities. Being at a 'meeting' has become a metaphor for being busy and hard at work for administrators and civil servants.

As the level of responsibility increases within the administration, fewer decisions are actually made. Making decisions can be a very risky business. By making decisions you can make mistakes or sometimes hurt the interests of an individual who, in all likelihood, is a member of a powerful afno manchhe circle. Doing something means taking responsibility for it, and when something is done badly, then failure is attributed to incompetence. To keep an administrative position for as long as possible, the best strategy is to act as little as possible, so that the danger of dismissal is diminished. A general rule for working in such a bureaucracy is: The lower you are the more active you are, because you have high aspirations and are working hard to realize them. The higher you are, the greater you are at risk and the less you do.

A variation of not doing work is to pass it up to a higher level. Decisions are being constantly deferred to the top, which , until recently, was ultimately the King. Alternatively, decisions can be passed on to a committee, thereby diffusing responsibility through collective action. Other practices, derived from the sense of fatalism, include recourse to such things as astrology, Shamanic divining and oracular practices, and priestly services. Such practices are evident at all levels of government, though they are done discretely and privately.

Sometimes there are jobs that have a pressing need to be completed, and at such times they do get done quickly. But most things happen casually rather than by conscious design.

*The Central Role of the King*

The Nepali word for government is 'Sarkar', and the same word is used as address and in reference to the king. 'Sarkar' is the equivalent the English 'Your Majesty.' Thus king and government are equivalent in the Nepali cultural-historical context. The king embodies government. The idea that the king and government are synonymous pervades Nepali attitudes towards government, politics, and the maintenance of law and order[1]. The relationship between the king and the government is solidly reinforced by another relationship, which is equally important. This is the relationship between king and state. The Nepali word for king and state are 'Raja' and 'Rajya' respectively. The word rajya is derived from the word raja, so state government and king are aspects of the one and the same thing. They are inseparable.

The relationship between the king and the people has always been harmonious, in large part because the people treat their king as a father figure who protects the interests of his children. In fact, the king is also often called 'father.' The father connection is an important one, derived ultimately from the pervasive paternal dependency that so characterizes certain sections of Nepali society. Such dependency ensures a high degree of stability in Nepal, at least with regard to the people's relations with the king. It also permeates the vertical structure of society and the administrative hierarchy within the government, which might be best characterized as an overlapping series of paternal relations.

Genuine authority is always with the king, who thus becomes the central focus for chakari. Throughout the various attempts at establishing alternate forms of political assembly, from psuedo-parliamentary to the Panchayat systems, and in the various experiments with democracy, the king has always remained the ultimate power, and at times has been forced to exercise this power. But while having such power, the king has never been autocratic. Since the Ranas, each king has been favorable to democratic attempts and has intervened only at the point of crisis, much as a father would. He is also the repository of shifted responsibilities, particularly from the administrative bureaucracy. During the Panchayat period an important practice of senior civil servants, who constitute collectively the working arm of the government, was to establish as close a relationship with the king as possible. The observations made by Rose and Fisher about the administrative machinery two decades ago still reflects the situation today:

> The decision-making process continues to be highly confused, and the locus of responsibility for decisions is often difficult to determine. The enlarged administrative structure and the more complex nature of the problems

> with which the government is now concerned make it virtually impossible for the King to function effectively in the style of the Rana Prime Ministers but, in essence, that is what is expected of him. No other official is prepared or, indeed, is in a position to assume responsibility for even comparatively minor matters which can more safely be pushed to the palace for a final decision. Where this is not feasible, the tendency is to form ad hoc committees within the Central Secretariat to consider a question, thus reducing individual responsibility but slowing down the decision-making process (Rose and Fisher, 1970: 67-68).

The deep seated paternal dependency of the Nepali character is a reality that cannot be ignored. These structural features of a national character have consequences on the ideal forms of social organisation of a culture. Alien social organisations can rarely accomodate these peculiarities of a national character and may result in the kind of conflict experienced by Nepal when it introduced the Western parliamentary system through India in the fifties. With time, the structure of these imported organisations has to be adapted to the national character. An example is the peculiarly Chinese adaptation of the communist system. In Nepal, any imported political system must be adapted to accomodate the demands of paternal dependency.

When an attempt was made to introduce a parliamentary system in the fifties, something else evolved in its place; the Panchayat System. But to a large extent this, too, remained merely a formal political structure and as was proven by the recent revolution a formal structure is not necessarily the most appropriate one. While the panchayat system was evolving, so, too, was an extensively informal and absolutely corrupt political apparatus around the King.

The King had his own personal secretariat at the palace and each secretary acted as a link between the concerned ministry and the King. Formally, these secretaries had no power. Informally, the secretaries were more powerful than the civil secretaries and the ministers, and were often deferred to by individual bureaucrats, at least until the Panchayat System collapsed in April 1990. Essentially, they acted as ombudsmen, cementing the inadequacies of the Panchayat-bureaucratic system. The largest number of chakariwals in the country came to these secretaries.

King Birendra developed the practice of moving himself to different parts of the country, with his secretaries, for one month every year, during the winter. The King was thus made visible to the people throughout the country and, in attending to their problems while travelling, demonstrated to them that he was a real force in Nepal. For the common person, the National Panchayat remained an abstraction. During these regional visits, the King's secretaries met with regional chakariwals and this has had a significant impact on development in these regions. On such visits a minister-in-waiting from the National Panchayat was always present with the King to 'carry the orders of the King' to the Cabinet if he should so desire. Sometimes, he took the Prime Minister or particular ministers or secretaries with him. The net impact of this was to demonstrate to the people that, (a) the King was really concerned for their well being; (b) he could really do things for them; and (c) the National Panchayat and Prime Minister defer to him and were of secondary importance.

*Democracy in Nepal*

No sensible person would deny that the most important aspect of democracy is equality in opportunity and rights. Currently, in Nepal, it is the educated Hindu high caste who have most of the opportunities, and their natural tendency, consciously and unconsiously, is to protect these privileges. The majority of the people need a democracy in which their interests are constantly considered and expanded, while the stratified hierarchy of the caste system is abolished completely. But since the common people are not the ones who clamour for political power, and show little interest in the tools of aggressive class action, either by being members of political parties or through strikes, they are misunderstood by the educated elites who consider politics as the decisive factor in social change.

The term democracy covers a multitude of political forms. For some it connotes particular kinds of determined social action. Some associate it with lofty ideals of liberty and equality and believe it means emulating the activists of the French Revolution to topple the exclusively privileged through fervent mass movements and rallies. Others confine it to party politics, where minority interests are identified, consolidated, represented and defended against those of other minorties. But the path to social change must not only accommodate but should strongly resonate with the cultural requirements of the people, and many of the political forms that have been promoted in Nepal reflect social organizations that are essentially alien. The kind of democracy envisioned by some to be successful would require the elimination of the social fabric of the Nepali society and its replacement by the psychology to act in an independent and self-assertive fashion.

Democracy in Nepal must recognize the collective orientation of the people as well as the ubiquitous and multiple forms of paternal dependency. This paternal dependency could readily lead to the development of a polity which is essentially antagonistic to the genuine interests of the people because it is supportive of various forms of authoritarianism and of the cumbersome form of government by bureaucracy that has currently evolved. While the democratic needs of the people have to be met their need for beneficient guidance and nurturance has also to be realized. Ultimate authority in Nepal must reside with a power which can recognize both the needs and can be committed to the genuine interests of the people. Unless Nepal is able to maintain an institution which can develop this kind of commitment it would be an extremely difficult job to lead a plural society through the process of rapid growth and economic development. At the same time a constant evaluation of progress made towards the desired goal is an absolute necessity to remain on course.

An immediate requirement is undisturbed effort at economic development and an expansion of proper educational facilities. The country could not pick up any developmental momentum after the Rana family rule, because of the lack of a genuine leadership and the predisposition of those in positions of authority to slip back into the old ways of doing things. Since then there have been experiments with different types of political systems. But the people have much to learn before a representative system can work properly, and in particular they need to learn to bear responsibility and work hard to develop skills and self-confidence for self government.

For a long time to come, the position of the monarch as a symbol of unity and national sovereignty will be very important and crucial in the development of a national society which comprises so many different ethnic, cultural and linguistic communities. Nepalis will have to learn to shoulder responsibility, develop an open mind to respect each other as equals and help bring about a change in their basic attitude of fatalism, so that they have an appreciation of the fact that things change only as a result of hard and determined individual action. Instead of blaming others for not shouldering responsibility and waiting for someone else to act on their behalf, they need to try to do things for themselves. For generations Nepalis have been promised the beautiful imaginary land of *swarga* (heaven), where everything comes true miraculously without having to make any effort, and where they can reserve a place for themselves by paying an advance to the priests, who act like reservation clerks in a travel agency. The worst part is that the job is not carried out by a person who was trained to be a priest but by a Bahun individual who considers it his privilege by being born in a Bahun family.

Democratic culture cannot be institutionalised simply by the preachings of erudite scholars. They must adopt this as a way of life for themselves to begin with. Only when Nepalis have internalized responsibility for themselves and accepted the need to liberate themselves from cultural mores that threaten loss of status for working productively, will the groundwork be established for a different and more developed form of democracy.

## NOTES AND REFERENCES

1 For example, many common people, when they suffer injustice, use the expression 'Alas! The king cannot see it and God who sees it does not speak' (Raja dekhtaina, dekhne deuta boldaina).

CHAPTER SIX

# EDUCATION

The ministry of education in Nepal is currently one of the largest ministries in the government, with a large budget. An investigation into its operation will provide an opportunity for a close examination of the operation of government in Nepal. Through it we can get an idea of the working of Nepali bureaucracies and how policy is formulated and applied. Education itself is also of critical importance in the study of development because it is through education that the nation's manpower resources are improved and the various skills necessary for development acquired. The chapter begins with a consideration of the traditional attitude towards education in Nepal and examines the development of the educational system since the Rana period.

*Education in the Past*

In earlier days, particularly during the Licchavi period, Kathmandu Valley society clearly had a substantial body of highly skilled and professional labourers, including engineers and architects. Their skills were demonstrated not only within Nepal, but also in Tibet. These accomplishments were acquired in relatively sophisticated educational institutions, perhaps modelled on the great universities of the plains at Taxila, Pataliputra, and Nalanda. During this period, most of the institutions of higher education were Buddhist and, perhaps, the Nepali institutions were Buddhist as well. Buddhist institutions generally seem to have been well supported by the Licchavi government. Today, no direct evidence for such institutions exists but, given the power and significance of Nepali society at that time, and the fact that Nepal was a source of engineering, metallurgy, and architectural skills, they probably did exist along with an indigenous scientific and literary heritage. Tibetan and Chinese documents from that period also suggest such a probability.

The advent of the Sankaracharya in the eleventh century seems to mark a turning point for these educational resources in Nepal. Buddhist institutions were attacked and the products of their work destroyed, with widespread book-burnings. These included not only religious texts, which may have been seen as rivalling Sankaracharya's version of Saivitic thought, but also other secular literature, works of grammar and dictionaries. Few written works other than administrative edicts carved in stone exist from this period. Nepali literary history begins, for us, only in the fourteenth century. If a written literary and scientific heritage did exist in the Licchavi period it must have been destroyed in the Sankaracharya conflagration, and we might also expect that Buddhist and other non-Saivitic educational institutions were destroyed at the same time. Certainly, nothing survives of them.

While this surmise of an early institutional educational apparatus is highly speculative, it is probable. Its form would have been determined by Buddhist organizational practices, which tended towards creating regulated schooling systems and some centres of higher education, usually connected with the monasteries. The Hindu system of education was quite different from that of the Buddhist; the model was that of the *gurukul*, with prime emphasis on the *guru* (teacher) *shishya* (pupil) relationship. Often, as was the case in Nepal, the role of guru was assumed by the father, thereby compounding the special qualities of the father-son relationship. Education traditionally consisted of learning, ritual, prayer, and the reading of religious texts. To be educated one had to be born into a caste where such an education was appropriate. Education ceased to be the means of acquiring practical skills. Its connection with productive activity, such as with engineering applications, dissappeared and was replaced with this more narrow orientation towards ritual life. With time, education ceased to have relevance for the majority of the population who had to work for a living. Eventually Sanskrit schools, or Sanskrit Pathsalas, were introduced for high caste children, and the father's role as teacher was diminished, though not eliminated. Fathers still taught their children up to their entry to Sanskrit Pathsalas and, often, children were literate in

Sanskrit by the time they went to school. Most high caste children went to such schools though, in some instances, the tradition of the father as guru persisted.

The Sanskrit Pathsalas were funded out of guthi, or the grants and gifts donated to them by both the government and devout private parties. The nature of these grants allowed much independence from the government, so that the pathsalas were autonomous bodies. Pathsala resources varied with the size of the guthi. These schools were boarding schools and were divided into primary grades (prathama, ages 7-8), and middle grades (madhyama, ages 13-16). The schools taught mostly Sanskrit texts, puranas and ritual documents. Graduation from a pathsala had little direct meaning, there was little to distinguish the pathsala trained and those who had been taught by their fathers. The most important ideal for the high caste student was to gain admission to the Sanskrit college at Benares. Admission there was dependent on passing an examination to which both pathsala and home trained students were eligible. Those who were able to go to Benares came back with the highest prestige, as all pundits were initially from there.

For high caste people, teachers were available to teach religious texts and ensure a basic literacy, necessary for purposes of administration. In the education of upper-class and or caste students, bound for careers in the government as experts in foreign affairs, Moghul influence became apparent. Urdu and Persian were introduced and taught from the nineteenth century.

*Education under the Ranas*

During the Rana period (1847-1950), the British system of education, as practised in India, began to have some influence. Soon after the Ranas came into power, the first school was founded by Jung Bahadur Rana within the confines of the Rana's palace, as part of a modernization programme initiated after a visit to France and England. The palace school was accessible only to Rana children. From the beginning, there was an awareness of the potential of the educational system as an instrument of change, so that an attempt was made to control its effects by keeping the school under close scrutiny. After Jung Bahadur's death, his successor, Ranoddip Singh Rana became prime minister. He was more liberal and moved the school from the palace grounds and opened it to other non-Rana children of high status.

This school, called Durbar (Palace) High School, was one of the first of what came to be known as the English schools. These English schools consisted of nine grades, with enrolment beginning at the age of seven or eight. Though the school was theoretically open to all, in effect it remained open only to those in the Rana family and the upper class close to them. The curriculum was derived from the English model and included courses in English, mathematics, history and geography. While Nepali and Sanskrit were taught, little else of Nepal was introduced. The history or geography that was taught was confined to that of the British Isles and India, a practice that was to instil a sense of inferiority and ineffectiveness of things Nepali and a debasement of the ethnic heritage of the different Nepali peoples. For the next forty years no other schools were added or opened.

Those educated in the Durbar High School became valued by the Ranas because of their knowledge and skills that became increasingly important for dealing with the outside world, both politically and economically. All graduates of the school were employed by the Ranas in some administrative capacity. Eventually, a school education became a prerequisite to employment in various important government positions and came to symbolize power and prestige.

Some of the educated began to think of the future of Nepal and the place of education within it. One such idealist was Dev Shumsher Rana, who became prime minister after the death of his elder brother, in 1901. He started opening up primary schools throughout the country. Almost two hundred schools were opened before his younger brother, Chandra Shamsher, exiled him after four months in office. The wary attitude of the Ranas towards education was still evident, and these new schools were soon closed down under suspicion of being instruments of treason.

Subsequently, another kind of school, a Nepali language pathsala or Bhasha Pathsala, was developed during the Rana period. Its purpose was to train students in clerical skills, to become clerks in the Rana administration, typically in positions beneath those produced by the Durbar High School. It was open to all, though mainly high caste male children went there. These schools were funded by the state and not by guthi, and hence were not autonomous as the Sanskrit Pathsalas were.

In 1947, when India attained Independence from British rule, several Basic Schools on the principles of Mahatma Gandhi were founded. As interpreted in Nepal, these principles emphasized productive self-sufficiency. This focus on skills training and commitment to work was never really popular and these schools failed to attain the prestige of the Durbar High School. This innovation had been introduced by yet another liberal Rana prime minister, Pudma Shumsher, who was later forced to resign and enter self-exile. For a short time the momentum for educational expansion was arrested, but to have Independence in India was an impact on Nepal.The Ranas were soon removed, and the educational movement resumed.

The first college in Nepal was founded in 1918, with its students recruited from Durbar High School. Courses in economics, civics (political science), English literature, history, geography, Nepali and Sanskrit literature, mathematics, physics and chemistry were offered. The professional quality of the graduates of the college, however, was not high. Some Rana students, or those close to the Ranas, were sent out of the country, to Japan, Europe, or India, for professional education in such disciplines as medicine and engineering.

The Ranas designated a Director-General of Public Education but it was essentially an impressive title with little responsibility. Mostly, the Director-General was available to listen to complaints. Other officers of importance who were responsible for education under the Ranas included the Inspector of Schools, who checked on the quality of education in both English and Pathsala schools, and the college Principal's Office, whose sole concern was the administration of the college. Funds for the English Schools were provided by the Prime Minister's office, rather than by the Director-General. The Public Construction Office was responsible for the provision of school buildings, while building maintenance was the responsibility of yet another office. Both the high school and college curricula were developed at Patna, in India.

On the whole, there was no real educational policy and the functions of educational administration were dispersed and uncoordinated. The educational system produced recruits for the government, typically for communication with foreign powers. Most professionals in Nepal, at that time, whether doctors, engineers or architects, were not the products of the Nepali educational system but were graduates of Indian schools.

*Early Fifties*

There were some sporadic efforts to develop and modernize the country during the pre-1950 period, but real concerted programmes were introduced only after 1950. Activity in the government sector began to expand rapidly, creating both white and blue collar jobs at a dramatic rate. People with marginal qualifications could find attractive jobs and this began to have a profound impact on the people at large. Enrolment at existing schools and colleges began to swell beyond their capacities, causing more such institutions to come into being. But there was still no widespread sense of the general importance of education for the country as a whole, and there was only a very primitive kind of educational policy. People did not look for any benefit from education apart from the assurance of white collar jobs, which they expected to be provided in unlimited numbers.

As discussed in the previous chapter, when the Ranas were overthrown the model of government adopted was imported from India. A Minister of Education was appointed, with political credentials, whose task was to build the first ministry. The development of a real ministry, along Indian lines, lead to a bureaucratization of the educational civil service, with a great increase in size of the administrative machinery. The increased bureaucracy allowed an expansion of opportunities for the educated, as they now had a greater number of government positions to fill.

Success in gaining a prestigious position within the government administration now depended on having the appropriate formal qualifications as well as having the right afno mannche connections. The most highly regarded qualification was the Bachelor's Degree, which allowed one to qualify for any government job. Next in importance came the high school diploma which qualified the recipient for lower clerical jobs. None of these qualifications prepared the person for the job to which he was attached, but were merely formal degrees. For a time, in the 1950's, formal qualifications, and especially a certificate of graduation, became the significant factor for acquiring a job. This affected the general educational process by promoting a 'certificate orientation' at the cost of the quality of education.

The main impetus for change in the realm of education at that time came not from the ministry or from the existing school and college system but from the initiative of the people. The motivation to improve the school system was based on the fact that education had become a necessary requisite for certain jobs and had become a symbol of prestige in itself. During the Rana period, education in the English Schools was the privilege of the higher-classes. The opening of English Schools was seen by some as a door to higher class status. Nepalis who had been to India, or even further, were impressed by the contribution of education to modernization and were ready to support changes in the educational system.

It was mainly the upper caste people who pushed for educational expansion. With the overthrow of the Ranas there was a re-emergence of hope and pride, manifested in aspirations for important social and political positions through education. The upper caste people dispersed throughout Nepal were mainly members of the entrepreneurial middle class, acting as local money lenders and eventually landlords and patrons of the local clients. They used local funds and resourcess to build schools, based on the 'English' model, only for the purposes of educating their own children. Schools were rarely opened specifically for local ethnic people as, in the early years, they were not interested in sending their children to such schools. Only after the school commenced at the local level was there an attempt to acquire formal state recognition, and perhaps state support. To some extent, the self-initiated local activity was meant to act as a 'lure' to the government; providing the initial local educational infrastructure that might elicit a greater willingness to action on the part of the Kathmandu authorities. It was at this point, however, that these local groups encountered the ineffectiveness of the formal bureaucratic machinery and were forced to make new approaches to the central educational authorities as chakariwals. One consequence was the further strengthening of the chakari system in the new regime.

Today most of the educated come from the upper caste and upper class groups dispersed throughout the country. Most local ethnic groups still feel the need for higher education although an increasing number of their children are attending the primary schools that have been opened throughout the country.

*Later Fifties and Sixties*

Things began to change further in the field of education when the United States extended both technical and financial resources to the government of Nepal from 1954. Many people, inside and outside Kathmandu, were suspicious of American motives and this suspicion was exacerbated by Marxist-oriented political groups. Initially, many schools built with local initative wanted no connection with the American programme. But in course of time, American influence came to be the most significant in educational development. The American advisors were instrumental, along with the Ministry of Education, in organizing a National Educational Planning Commission (NEPC) in March 1954 to survey the state of education and present a general report on the educational needs of the country. They founded the first college of education, including a 'demonstration school' for the training of teachers, and the Normal Schools, which were mobile training schools for primary school teachers.

American efforts were also directed to help develop Multipurpose High Schools in various parts of the country, with an emphasis on technical training. New colleges, founded at this time, were the result mainly of Nepali efforts with little American participation. American assistance helped train many Nepalis at American universities and helped organize the first university in Nepal. Tribhuvan University was founded in 1956.

During the late fifties and the sixties, the school system was expanded and opened to a greater range of people. The initiative remained community based and schools tended to remain very small. To be approved, local schools had to follow the government approved curriculum. Pathsala Schools continued to provide free education to Bahuns of priestly background.

During this period, the bureaucracy of the Ministry of Education grew considerably. It was highly centralized, though organized on a regional basis. Small regional offices existed to distribute the meagre amounts of money provided by the state, inspect levels of performance, and grant permission to open new schools. The Ministry was conceived to have a large planning responsibility from the beginning, but there was little real planning and Ministry functions focused on recruitment, general and fiscal administration.

Many people realized that the educational system was meaningless, and not geared to the special needs of the country. Education was quickly becoming a symbol of status, as high school and college diplomas and degrees were being used simply for the purpose of acquiring higher status. The bureaucratic organization of the ministry quickly ossified; planning was reduced to acts of punditry; and chakari became, once more, the established way of getting things done. Though school and college graduation was necessary for job advancement, it still required the development of the correct afno mannche to secure one's position, and in the final analysis afno mannche was the critical element and not job skills or qualifications. Exposure to western culture and technology acted to illuminate the disparity between Nepal and the technically advanced nations, which tended to feed the Nepali sense of inferiority. For many, this sense of inferiority merely fed the belief in fatalism. The task of transforming Nepali society into one technically and economically at par with the rising Asian standard became daunting and a common response was passive resignation. The belief in fatalism encouraged this response. But some of those who did not ascribe to this fatalistic belief system responded differently. Within this marginal group there developed a stronger sense of the need for a developed manpower base and the critical role of education within it. This concern then led to demands for stronger technical education — demands that ran counter to the prevailing tendencies, and which, therefore, were implicitly seen as antagonistic to those supporting the ascriptive model for Nepalese society. The result was the National Education System Plan (NESP).

*National Education System Plan*

The initiative for educational change came from the centre of the power structure, King Mahendra himself, and made it easier for those interested in developing manpower resources through education to overcome opposition from conservative sections of society. The government was able to prepare and execute a national education system plan by 1969. The educated elite accepted this change rather reluctantly, and felt that it was unfairly imposed on them by a powerful minority. From the beginning the change towards the technical orientation in education was challenged as undemocratic and, ironically, a western concept of democracy was used to defend a value system that is at the heart of a rigidly hierarchical caste system. Before the introduction of NESP, educational expansion was never based on the perceived needs of the common people but was designed only for those at the highest level of society. When it was extended downwards it never shed its elitist bias.

By the time the NESP was implemented there was, relatively, a larger number of educated Nepalis participating in policy formation as compared to 1954 when the NEPC was formed. All schools were nationalized with the exception of the Sanskrit Pathsala. All schools were fully supported by the government, and to support this new activity there was a large increase in the educational budget, with the Ministry of Education becoming one of the largest within the government. Actual changes were tested in a process of experimentation, carried out districtwise, and educational reforms were phased in gradually. However, new schools were still established as a response to local initiative and chakari and afno mannche were operative in getting things done at the local level. The implementation of NESP itself proved as yet another example of the successful operation of chakari and afno manchhe. The only sincere people involved in this exercise were the king and the crown prince, a young idealist who had just completed his education in western universities.

The fact that NESP was pushed rather prematurely became more than obvious in subsequent years. Its strong supporters themselves displayed their unhappiness with it by either sending their own children to schools not operating under NESP or by challenging its effectiveness when their own children did not succeed in getting admissions into the institutions they wanted, especially those which provided degrees in social sciences with little effort. This double standard and the practice of chakari to seek favours from the then Crown Prince, who was mainly responsible for the introduction of NESP, became increasingly clear. NESP thus began to lose its efficacy and strength as soon as its former supporters turned out to be its saboteurs.

Meanwhile other changes were made within the colleges and the university, including the introduction of entrance examinations and a semester system. The system of examinations was overhauled so that, for the first time, students had to work hard at their studies and demonstrate their academic competence on a regular basis. This was different from the previous system of annual examinations. In order to gain a post-graduate degree, candidates were required to spend a year in rural areas, either working within local Panchayat organizations involved in development activities or teaching in a school. Though there was some initial resistance, eventually the students began to appreciate this. The programme proved to be so successful that it attracted the attention of other Third World countries.

As mentioned, the Ministry of Education was greatly expanded. As part of this expansion a National Education Committee was established under the chairmanship of the Education Minister which concentrated on the administration of education under his direct leadership. Previously, he had a more ineffectual role. This new position allowed the full realization of the paternal form of organization within the ministry. While there was an expansion of the middle level bureaucracy and a greater dispersion of the administrative apparatus across the country, the promotion of the Minister into what became a paternal role merely encouraged the tendency to bypass the bureaucracy and to concentrate chakari at the head of the organization.

The NEC in its formal plans set targets for the number of graduates in various specialized areas. Essentially, these targets proved to be unrealistic and pressurised both students and teachers, who soon reacted. Others voiced fear of sabotage of the local panchayat system by students in the NDS programme. The requirement of examinations threatened the system of privileges by emphasizing on competence. Some of those in higher positions became concerned that their own children might not be able to achieve the same status if they were to fail entrance examinations. Previously, their positions were guaranteed by social status and afno manchhe connections, but with the imposition of entrance examinations this was no longer the case. As the failures from the higher status increased, so, too, did the demands for the aboition of examinations. Students sabotaged the examination system through widespread and large-scale cheating, which was frequently ignored by supervisors and teachers. Cumulatively, there was enough opposition to ensure the demise of the NESP system. The entrance examination was the first reform to be discarded, and slowly the most effective parts of the system were dismantled. The NESP collapsed by 1979. What replaced the NESP was not the product of policy or of any commission, but merely a default system which was largely a reversion to the earlier form.

The legacy of NESP is the large educational budget, the increased power of the Education Minister and the large job providing bureaucracy, many parts of which no longer have any purpose as the programmes for which they were created have been abolished. The NDS system does continue in a reduced form, but it has been made almost irrelevant. There is much cheating to fulfil requirements and little serious labour. Polytechnic Schools, providing technical skills, have been developed as optional schools open to anyone finishing the eighth grade. Skills training itself is becoming increasingly popular, and, in particular, women's technical schools, providing training in nursing, and home science, are well attended.

Nepal has made impressive progress by any standards during the past four decades. The literacy rate was two per cent in 1951 and has now reached over forty per cent. Eighty-five per cent of all children of school going age are at school. A target of sixty per cent literacy has been planned with primary education for all by the end of the century. Women's literacy has been rather slow with only twelve per cent of the total in 1986. In 1986 nearly eighty per cent of all children aged 6-10 were in primary schools; thirty-one per cent aged

11-12 were in lower secondary schools; and twenty-three per cent aged 13-15 were in secondary schools. This amounted to more than 2,700,000 students in 18,688 schools from primary to higher secondary levels. There were 77,844 teachers. There are currently more than 150 campuses including private ones, a university faculty of more than 4000, and an equal number of administrative staff. Admission of students at college level had reached more than 80,000 in the year 1988-89. More than 18,000 students have been admitted to science colleges and in technical institutes during the same period. The figures are impressive but they belie the abuse and misapplication of educational qualifications, the minimal real impact that education has had in extending the manpower resources of the country, the extensive laxity in discipline combined with cheating that is undermining academic standards, and the administrative chaos that is currently rampant within the university system. What does exist has been due, in large part, to community-based initiative.

The reason that a considerable number of children do not attend school is that they form a major portion of the economic workforce. In a majority of cases, where agriculture is the main subsistence, children have to play an active role in augmenting the workforce of the family. Sometimes this goes beyond family level and their working hours have to be pooled for the general need of the entire community or village. Children in such situations collect all the cattle of the village, take them to a common grazing area and look after them while adult members of the village are busy with agricultural work during the peak seasons. There is also the practice of requisitioning female children's labour from the schoolroom, so that boys remain in school longer than the girls throughout rural Nepal. Even in the suburban areas of Kathmandu and among the poorer sections in urban areas, girls drop out of school much earlier than boys though both sexes are sent to school at the same age. Children are part of a continuous extension of the economic and social life of society and circumstances still greatly restrict their opportunities for education.

Because, traditionally, education was designed solely for the high caste and highly placed people, the newly educated people tend to equate themselves with these classes. That is why we have so many educated people who do not want to work. Education has made them socially equal with prosperous people. The educated consider themselves purer and of higher status than those who are uneducated and who perform physical work. The educated are just as loathe to work physically and productively as are traditionally high caste people. With the increasing popularity of modern education there is also a proportionate dislike for work and an increasing dependency on external help, influential connections, the institutionalization of chakari and the practice of nepotism and favouritism for self-promotion. In fact, passing the grades in the school in a large part of the country is considered more important than acquiring skills or knowledge.

Technical education lags far behind what is necessary for the country to meet its developmental goals. Various skills practised at the working people's level continue to come from family-based, informal 'learning-by-doing'. This has never been recognized as a system of training by the government, even though this is the most widely practised method and has provided the large number of skilled or semi-skilled workers required by the country. The economy and the system in general have been sustained mainly by this group of productive people.

The majority of Nepalis do not have many job choices since occupation is determined by birth. For caste people this means an ascriptive determination of occupation, and for the non-caste people a determination by other cultural and economic circumstances. In either case, people are not accustomed to thinking of a choice of profession but learn, from generation to generation, the same professions from elders within the family. Nepalis in general do not believe that they have to be trained in anything beyond what they see and learn while assisting senior members of their own family. In cases where this is reasonably profitable there is no stigma attached and they are happy with their work, guarding their family or caste-based professional skills jealously. Technical professions have no traditions of training at formal institutions within Nepal but are taught, typically, within the family. All craftsmen today who perform professional jobs, such as masons, carpenters, bricklayers, bronze and other metal workers, mechanics, jewellers, weavers, and even agricultural workers, have never been formally trained. Not only the cobblers, tailors, iron and goldsmiths, potters and so forth, are born into the professional castes but even physicians and surgeons learn their skills while assisting their family members and do not consider formal training an essential part of the preparation for the job.

Alternate professions are not available outside of those prescribed by the circumstances of birth. The idea of occupational mobility is novel to Nepal and not strongly internalized. The education system has only recently been available to provide the opportunities for such occupational mobility. This new mobility has been largely in one direction, towards politics and administrative jobs which are considered to be the only respectable professions. These two fields are the only ones, outside priesthood, which could be undertaken without the risk of losing hierarchic caste position. Consequently, these occupations have acquired a lot of prestige and are associated particularly with high caste in the people's imagination. These professions are also the only ones where non-high caste people can work at the same level as the thread-wearing high caste, so that they are seen as a means of acquiring status. Becoming a politician or an administrator is, through association, synonymous with status mobility.

Technical trades have no real status and hence do not appeal to Nepali youth today when choosing their occupation. The qualifications gained in pursuing a technical degree, however, are valid qualifications for political and administrative positions, and it is only because of this that students become interested in technical education. The purpose of going to the technical school is to acquire the qualifications needed for entering the administration, not to acquire the skills needed to pursue some technical professional activity. Many people are not working in the technical professions for which they were formally trained, including those educated at universities abroad. Instead they go in for politics and administrative jobs. In the minds of such people there never was any interest or commitment to the jobs for which they were trained.

Technical schools have a long way to go before they can begin to make a visible impact on the national workforce in the manner intended. Membership in traditional professions was responsible for the social designation of vaishya, shudra, or untouchable status. The social objective of Nepali youth is to escape these denigrated categories and become neo-Bahuns. To do this they must actively avoid becoming professional technicians. Though there is a pressing need for skilled technicians and the technical institutes and schools to train them, the low regard for technical activity and the continuing strength of Bahun values compelled the government to establish a Sanskrit University recently, at the expense of the further improvement of other educational establishments.

The irony of the situation is that workers from lower social and economic levels gain status by assuming the role of the technically trained higher officials while the properly trained and qualified technical people lose status by working. Effectively, it is the unskilled low caste worker who has to do the job of the engineer, as well as fill the majority of the health posts outside Kathmandu and to administer first-aid and the distribution of medicine, as most of the time, trained health personnel are not available. An anthropological field researcher gives a vivid picture of the situation when she writes that:

> After walking several hours to reach a health post, I frequently arrived just as patients do, to find the health worker away, sometimes for a day, more often for several days—supervising village health workers (VHWs) in the fields, on official business in the district or center, or on personal leave. The peon (a formally untrained person employed in every office to do janitorial work and other menial jobs) remained at the post alone, informally interviewing and diagnosing patients, though he was not supposed to distribute medicine in the health assistant's absence. In each of the twenty-four health posts and ten hospitals I visited, I found peons actively involved in health care and in nine cases the peon was the only health worker available. A health inspector in western Nepal reported in September 1978 that three of the eight posts had trained health workers; the other five were staffed only by peons (Justice, 1986:101)[1].

There are few chances that a job will actually be performed by the person formally qualified to do it. This is clearly illustrated by the attempts at introducing modern technology into agriculture. Agricultural training institutions are built yet farmers are not the ones who go there for training. People who have no interest in the soil are the ones who get degrees in agricultural sciences. Graduation is regarded as the final hurdle in establishing rights over salaried positions within government. A university degree is considered a licence to reach the top of the social hierarchy and these people would not wish to lower themselves to the level of shudra by soiling their hands; the actual agricultural work is done by people who never get any training.

The national need for manpower skills has increasingly dominated the thinking of educational planners at the higher levels and the various training schools were established to produce these skills. Initially, few were interested in attending such schools and institutes so that a stipend had to be introduced to attract students. It was this stipend that was attractive, not the training program itself. As a result the wrong people have been trained with the best of intentions.

NOTES AND REFERENCES

1 Peons are usually from the clean castes who have gained their position through afno manchhe. In the health fields, such peons do learn medical skills informally, from their associations with the trained staff and other experienced peons.

CHAPTER SEVEN

# FOREIGN AID AND DEVELOPMENT

Nepal has made impressive progress during the past forty years. A roadless country in 1950, Nepal has built more than 6,000 miles of properly paved highways; Royal Nepal Airlines flies to fifteen destinations in thirteen countries and seven foreign airlines fly into Nepal regularly. Almost three hundred thousand tourists other than Indians visited Nepal during 1988 — a country which was closed to outsiders until 1950[1]; exports in 1987 were worth more than 151 million U.S. dollars (World Development Report, 1989), and more than seventy-five per cent of this was earned by industrial products as compared to a little over ten per cent in 1960, as nearly ninety per cent of the exports used to be agricultural and unprocessed primary goods till then (Economic Survey 1987-88, HMG 1988). The GDP has risen consistently: from 2.28% in 1972-73, to 7% in 1987-88. This would not have been possible without foreign aid.

Nepal has historically been self-sufficient and the idea of foreign assistance is a new one. Nepalis may be poor by international standards but the Nepali peasants are self-sufficient and largely content. Because of their isolation from international affairs, Nepalis had no idea that they were relatively impoverished until a few decades ago. With an increasing awareness of the relative affluence of the western world and other benefits of modern technology a desire for a change in the economic base of the country has been felt. Along with it has also increased the awareness of being the poorest country of the world. This is beginning to destroy the gracefulness, charm, generosity and hospitality even among the rural people. So the improved condition of Nepal in statistical terms is not necessarily all positive. People are paying their prices in terms of some positive human values which once lost will not be that easy to reinstate for generations to come.

The Ranas were particularly disinterested in foreign aid since it represented, for them, an alien intrusion into their private domain. For the most part, they were content to let Nepal continue in isolation, with a perpetuation of an economic system which had been prevalent for some hundreds of years. Any change in the social system represented a possible destabilizing threat, since once the process of change started it might not be easily controlled by the Ranas. There was also concern that foreign aid was connected to colonialism, and that the relations with foreign governments established through the acceptance of aid could provide opportunities for a more surreptitious infiltration. Such caution went to extremes. Indeed, the Rana Prime Minister, Shri Maharaj Juddha Shamsher declined an offer of financial assistance from England and France during the earthquake disaster of January 1934 (Pandey, 1987: 304-5)[2].

With the overthrow of the Ranas, Nepal was ill prepared to meet the challenge of development shared by Third World countries after the Second World War. What it did not share with many of these countries were the positive legacies of past colonialism. Nepal had little sense of the outside world, no infrastructure to support development, and no trained manpower resources. Various foreign governments were willing to provide aid, but there was no effective indigenous administration available to determine the country's needs, accept and distribute this aid. Nepal was actually able to spend only less than sixty-five per cent of the total allocated development budget during the first five year plan period of 1956-61[3].

### *Fatalism, Dependency and Foreign Aid*

From the early days of Nepal's history, the idea of aid or assistance has been associated with religious activities. Rich people donated land and resources (guthi) to temples and monasteries. They spent money for the construction of temples, water supply systems, rest houses bridges, and paved roads to gain religious merit. Charity was reserved for the ascetic, Sannyasi, Buddhist Bhikshu, and Bahun, who were, supposedly, devoting their lives to religious activities aimed at the general welfare of society. But this had no genuine altruisitic intent. There are instances of poor and lazy individuals from high caste assuming the role of 'sannyasi' and begging under the pretext that it is a holy act. However, begging is not considered to be dignified, even by for the religious.

The notion of giving charity to the needy is not generally compatible with fatalistic thought one's circumstances are fatalistically determined, and a life of suffering is intended to either compensate for earlier misdeeds or prepare the self for some form of spiritual evolvement. The predicament of others is therefore something that should not be casually interfered with. Charity to the poor and needy, outside of what is religiously prescribed, is not a genuinely altruistic act but might be seen more as an act of atheistic arrogance and as being ultimately negative and even destructive.

The Nepali attitude to the idea of aid is greatly affected by this opinion of begging and charity. The high caste cultural outlook also contains other beliefs grounded in fatalism that qualify the Nepali attitude towards aid and towards planned development. Some are critical of foreign aid because they do not believe in the efficacy of the human hand in the process of development. There is at the core of the religious faith the belief that the development of the universe is cyclical and spontaneous. They believe in the four ages of Satya, Treta, Dwapar and Kali, the Golden, Silver, Copper and Iron ages respectively. The Hindu theory of creation tells us that at the end of the four yugas, which are called Kalpa, the Satya Yuga comes back again automatically. People do not have to do anything about this. That age will have an abundance of everything and people will be happy. The present age of Kali Yuga is bad, as it is part of the grand design. In this world view, attempts at change are looked upon as arrogance and presumption because the deity himself takes care to bring about the necessary changes in the world if he thinks fit.

Fundamentalist Hindus who believe in the divine origin of things do not want foreign aid to interfere with what is determined for society. Even if not vocal they tend to be very uncooperative towards foreign aid. Confusion and bewilderment in foreign aid administrators and advisers is frequently caused by this attitude of many Nepali officials. As part of a high caste educated behaviour people learn not to use the negative expression 'no' to anything. It is considered good manners to say 'yes' all the time in response to anything, even when they have absolutely no intention of fulfilling the commitment. Many Westerners are blatantly deceived by a gentle smile and a cheerful disposition of Nepali officials at high and responsible positions when they take things at the face value.

But the attitude to foreign aid is greatly affected by the Nepali sense of paternal dependency. Foreign aid donors are sometimes seen as father-surrogates. China, in particular, has been seen in the past as the father of Nepal, and for this reason there is little fear that China's actions with regard to Nepal would be anything but beneficent. When this passive paternal dependency is applied to foreign aid, the only active agent of development becomes the foreign party, who then must supply the resources, the administration, the imagination to plan, and the motivation to make it all work. If it does not work, then this foreign father-surrogate must assume the responsibility for its failure. As will be seen, while Nepalis are slow to thank their foreign benefactors, they are quick to attribute blame to them for a host of real and imagined ills, while they themselves maintain a childlike innocence. This behaviour makes some foreign aid administrators and experts adopt an arrogant and condescending attitude towards their Nepali counterparts which in turn causes a resentment towards foreign aid among some Nepalis. These various orientations to foreign aid, with all their inconsistencies cannot form a positive receptacle for foreign efforts to support Nepali development.

*Planning Problems*

The Nepali rate of progress has been commensurate with the level of motivation and the amount of productive labour invested in it. These have been low. Issues of motivation and the orientation to work have been considered above and in earlier chapters. Another problem is the capacity to plan with the levels of complexity required for the national level. A strong future orientation, we know, is already lacking. The tendency for planning activities to be divorced from the realities they are meant to address add to these complications.

Debate and argument is a respected activity for the educated and the delight in punditry extends to the bureaucracy.

But the substance of these arguments is abstract and metaphysical. The ideals expressed rarely have reference to things in the real world. At a philosophical level, truth is determined through a combination of linguistic virtuosity and religious authority, not because there is a determined correspondence between a derived proposition and some event in the real world. At a national level, Nepali thinking has not reached a stage of empiricism and pragmatism. The mentality of the Sanskritic tradition wherein education is totally divorced from any practical use and found useful only for distinctive social positions is not conducive to pragmatic programmes of economic development.

Planning involves the detailing and testing of the connections between resources, objects and events, and the determination of an efficient course of action to attain desired results. It involves economic (and social) modelling and strategic thought. Control is placed in the hands of the planner. But fatalism does not allow this kind of control, and is inherently antithetical to pragmatic thought. Under fatalism, control lies with the deity and with fate. Further, the responsibility that pragmatic planning imposes is too great for any Nepali to assume because they are mainly concerned about their own security and promotion which could be endangered by assuming such responsibilities. At this stage, very few behave as if they are capable of thinking and acting pragmatically. This state of affairs does not affect the conscience of the educated Nepalis, who know well that pragmatism is an essential ingredient of successful development, as its fits in with high caste behaviour and the principle of fatalism.

Over the past few decades, numerous Nepali students have travelled abroad to study in other countries, and have returned with advanced degrees in various professional capacities. Most of them come from high caste backgrounds. While visiting foreign places, they have been influenced by other cultures, and have learnt something of the values and psychology necessary for success in the modern world. Upon their return many are placed in positions of authority, as they represent the cream of Nepal's manpower resources. Though they may be initially inspired by a high degree of idealism, the new values that they bring back with them immediately confront fatalism and are typically defeated by it. Some return to their basic fatalistic beliefs. Some have a sense of what needs to be changed but are overwhelmed by the magnitude of the task, and simply surrender to their basic passivity and the belief that they cannot personally contribute to that change. Those who are strongly affected by their overseas travels are considered socially deviant. Few have been able to survive this hostility with their determination intact. The accomodations which they are compelled to make render many of their innovations irrelevant. Many feel forced to become expatriates. Those who remain become cynics and adapt to chakari and afno manchhe culture.

After forty years of planning and an accumulation of foreign trained graduates, Nepal, then, still has little manpower to effectively bridge the disparities between the culture of the foreign aid donors and that of her own. The foreign aid specialists are often insensitive to the peculiarities of the cultural system in Nepal, and do not incorporate these peculiarities into their developmental models, while the Nepalis are estranged from the actual intent of such aid and subvert it to irrelevant or personal ends.

Among those things that have been successfully imported are the modern bureaucratic forms and tools, adapted in Nepal to serve fatalistic functions. One of the most favoured is the seminar. It allows people an opportunity to demonstrate their erudition, and to rise in stature as modern pundits. The activity of these seminars is essentially a manipulation and play on words; real decisions are not made and real and effective actions are not undertaken.

The material upon which planning proceeds rarely involves important data germane to key developmental problems. Planners are mostly unfamiliar with the areas that they are working on, and fail to take the peculiarities of local geography into account. When a concrete action is taken it is often simply a response to the genuine planning initiative; begun at the local level, or in response to a political decision or an agreement made under the chakari system, which has been passed on to the planning bureaucracy as a directive. Enormous financial resources are devoted to bureaucratic planning with very little results. A former high level bureaucrat has even commented that, in spite of almost four decades of foreign assistance, agriculture has not benefited; the poor have been bypassed; the needs of women have not even been understood; the relations of production and distribution of power have become worse; and technical assistance has not contributed to the improvement of administrative capability (Pandey, 1983: 282).One of the senior bureaucratic officials of the National Planning Commission, himself a foreign university trained administrator, conceded that:

> There are more people today who have ability to plan, implement and evaluate programmes of development in the country. But whether they have the needed initiative, motivation and drive to do it on a continuing basis is what is questionable. One of the characteristic features of His Majesty's Government offices is that people...gather together in one of the several office chambers (during official working hours) and indulge in exchanging informations that may have anything to do with their job or profession...and their sense of security goes with the knowledge that they have their own people (afno manchhe) in important positions that can affect their well being in their job. (Shrestha, 1983: 233).

The regulation of foreign aid is also fraught with difficulties. Aid administration is not a unilateral process, but involves negotiation between the donor and Nepali officials and takes place in an international political climate.Donor countries are acting from a mixture of altruistic and political motives. The American Aid Projects in the early years were specifically designed to fight communism with the encouragement of the American system of education and agrarian reform. A quotation from Mihaly's work would illustrate this quite clearly:

> The maintenance of political stability is dependent in very large measure upon the capacity of these countries to improve the productivity and the status of the agricultural population. The weaknesses of the present economies of South Asia bear most heavily upon the agrarian population and under current conditions, the agrarian sector offers a major target for communist subversion. Therefore, the proposed programme of

> economic assistance is designed to bring about improvements in the status of the agricultural population... In a broad sense, all the proposed forms of economic assistance in South Asia can be classed as extension work. (The Mutual Security Programme for Fiscal Year 1952, US Government, Executive Branch; (Mihaly 1965:29).

Even when altruistic, the consequences of developmental support have political overtones, especially because of Nepal's strategic position in relation to the Asian superpowers. On several occasions this has been used to Nepal's advantage, as political jealousies between opposed powers have resulted in a degree of generosity that would otherwise be absent. The different motivations of the donor countries are not always consistent with the ideas of development for Nepal. Sometimes for their own reasons, funding and other resources may be provided for projects that assauge the needs of these donor countries, but which have little real relevance for Nepal.

There have been several controversies regarding road construction. Foreign concerns are that such roads can have a military use in time of war and this has influenced both support and rejection of particular projects, with one power vetoing proposals presented by another. Often, conflicting demands must be accommodated, and this can either be to Nepal's benefit as the recipient of an extravagant courting process, or to her detriment, as critical projects can be vetoed when they compromise the imagined interests of other foreign parties. Together, international interest and the direct intervention of close powers in the formation and execution of key developmental projects reinforce the Nepali tendency to perceive machinations of fate overriding individual intent in determining Nepal's future development.

Most aid projects provide jobs with special benefits, which end when the project is completed or withdrawn. Knowing that individual consultants and project schemes come and go in a relatively short time, a Nepali may agree to a programme that he knows is inappropriate for Nepal in order to ensure his own job security (Justice, 1986:44). Excepting a few, the Nepali agent does not necessarily assume the responsibility of his country's best economic, political, and social interests after the negotiations are over. The effort of ensuring that such an agreement is properly executed is quite divorced from the effort of ensuring that an agreement is signed. Responsibility, as was discussed in an earlier chapter, is rarely assumed by the individual, but is placed in the hands of others or on fate. The responsible agents in such an agreement are, from the Nepali point of view, most often the foreign aid donors themselves.

International interests in Nepal are not always of a political nature. There is a large altruistic element, and this element does aim to work in Nepal's best interests. At times it is hard for Nepali motivations to match this. Often, the Nepali criteria for the determination of the allocation of resources for developmental purposes are internally political, or have been compromised by the demands of chakari. This can and does result in absurd wastage and even misuse of funds. The Nepali foreign aid civil servant operates from Kathmandu, and is oriented to assuming that the Kathmandu Valley is the real hub of national life. The plight of ethnic villagers in remote places is hard to identify with, they are invariably of low status (which decreases the amount of consideration due to them), and the actual physical nature of their environment is largely unknown. Impressive engineering projects may be planned to appease national political concerns, even though the economics justifying such projects may be questionable and the geographic circumstances unfavorable. At such times, foreign aid agents have interceded to recommend alternate courses of action. In other situations, a blundered Nepali project might be seconded with a better foreign project that is more attentive to economics and geography.

Some major developmental activities which are funded and developed juxtapose culturally opposed social elements. A key example has to do with agriculture. There is a stated need to raise production levels in the agricultural sector and thereby raise the standard of living for more than ninety-five per cent of the people. But the people and institutions that have been recruited to spearhead this development are far from being appropriate. As mentioned in the chapter on education, many of the people who go to agricultural colleges have absolutely no interest in agriculture. Instead, they are hierarchic high caste people for whom agricultural labour, and work of any kind, is unthinkable. They attend such colleges because they have no alternative open to them to gain some form of academic qualification now needed to obtain a job within the government bureaucracy. Consequently, Nepal is training people who loathe agricultural work and hate soiling their hands with earth to become agricultural specialists who ought to form the vanguard of an agricultural revolution. What they learn is never applied. Instead these trained agriculturalists are lost to the bureaucratic process, bloat the size of the bureaucracy, which, because of its parasitism, makes further claims on the meagre financial resources of the country, and deflects money away from genuine investments. Statistics show that Nepal has an impressive number of agricultural specialists who could lead the country to realize its agricultural objectives. The truth is the opposite.

A good example is that of the Pokhara Crop System Development Project. The programme began in 1977 with the objective of developing an understanding of different kinds of cropping systems by conducting research on the farmer's fields with the active participation of the farmers. The target village has two major groups of people living there: the dominant Bahuns and the original Gurungs. Because of the social differences between the two, the Gurungs live higher up the slopes and are nearer to the forested area where they can maintain their livestock more easily. Of the families the project authorities selected for intervention, five are Bahun and only one is Gurung. The others, being used as a control group, who practice both old and traditional farming methods, are all Gurung. But the high caste people in this area do not plough or cultivate their land, and spend most of the day in the town gambling. They have no interest in the Project. Their lands are tilled by low status labourers. Consequently, at the time I visited the area, the entire project was wasted and the Gurung farmers alienated.

There is no system of constantly monitoring the progress of development, to find out how it affects the people. Government departments publish reams of progress reports detailing added facilities built through foreign aid, and these are used to suggest that impressive progress has been made. But the facts that figure in these reports, and that are included in formal developmental models, are devoid of any real social or human elements. There is a snowstorm of statistical wizardry without any inkling of how these abstract figures relate to the condition of the bulk of the people, particularly those outside Kathmandu. Buildings and bridges might be built but there are questions as to whether they will be used, how they will be used and to what constructive end.

*The problem of Local Orientation*

Nepal was a medieval state, run for the benefit of a single family. There was no developed national consciousness and no real national economy, but people were content with their village lives. For the bulk of the population, government was something at a distance, unconcerned with their welfare, preoccupied with its own remote self-interests. Occasionally, government officials might come by, but they would usually require some service or produce for the benefit of others, and never for the local people visited. Civil works of benefit to the villagers were undertaken by the village members cooperatively, under the leadership of the village headman and had nothing to do with Kathmandu. The government was mostly associated with an alien ethnic people, essentially foreigners, who were in political ascendance. When projects and people associated with foreign aid first came, people mistook them as the successors of the Ranas. It seemed as if another group of people from some distant place, speaking another language, were engaged in projects determined by them, for their own purpose. It suggested only a change in a remote regime, and nothing of direct personal consequence.

For the people, foreign aid has introduced various social concepts, the novelty of which has in turn moderated the intended impact of such aid. When the people's conception of society extends little beyond that of the village, notions of government, of the state, nation and patriotism, and of the people and the public, are often difficult to grasp. There is a concept of community, but it is a localized concept. In the villages people do have a private life, and they also have common grazing grounds, sometimes a special structure for holding community events, and community responsibilities. But the members of the community are directly identifiable, and its construct is concretely grounded in perceptible social actors. By contrast, the public, the state, the nation, are all abstract concepts.

More will be said about nationalism in the next chapter. What is of relevance at this point is the failure in the appreciation of the concept of public, particularly as it involves ownership. Often foreign aid will target a particular project. This might be a bridge, or a major building, or a road, or even something as dissimilar as the planting of an orchard. Such a project tends not to be determined with a local input, and the only participation of the local population is in terms of their paid labour. After completion, and when the foreign aid project directors have moved on, this new construction is left as a public property or a public convenience. But the connection between such public property and community ownership is rarely made in Nepal. The projects are not village endeavours, and are thought to be the whims of the foreign project directors. They belong to these foreign or outside parties and not to the village. The intellectual leap from community property to public property is not made. This is true not only of rural people but even urban people in Kathmandu. The piled up dirt and garbage, unclaimed cattle sitting in the main thoroughfare, sometimes in the best paved or brick-lined streets, speak for the missing connection between the two.

There are many instances of such foreign aid projects never being used because of this problem of ownership. Bridges get built, but the local villagers continue to manage a chasm and ford a stream, because they have always done so and they have no sense of the public ownership of the bridge. Foreign aid has now existed in Nepal for almost forty years, yet this behaviour is still widespread. People lack any sense of either pride or of possession of these projects as they would towards things they built through their own efforts. Some years ago, I made an evaluation of five village Panchayats inhabited by different ethnic people. There were a number of foreign aid projects on rural development carried out in all of them but most villagers were not appreciative of what had been done for them and consistently interpreted the projects as being executed for the satisfaction of the needs of the foreign project officials involved. In such villages the foreign experts remained outsiders for ever and left the place either unhappy, or indifferent.

I have made surveys in other villages where foreign volunteers have worked and lived with the local people. There are many instances where they were adopted by the families with whom they lived through the Tika festivals of Dasain and Tihar. In such cases they were not treated as foreigners and were frequently addressed in kinship terms. In such cases the foreign volunteers had become their afno manchhe and the local people felt obliged to take them, and anything they constructed seriously.

As mentioned earlier, much of the real initiative for change and development comes from the people themselves. These locally initiated projects, when funded by the central authorities, have the greatest chance of success. The local people then understand the purpose of the project and what it means to them, because of their involvement from the beginning. They have a committment to the project, the results of which are recognised as belonging to them, and which they can then utilize and make productive. When the project engineers, if any, move on, there is a local agency with a vested interest in the upkeep or even improvement of the project. The project is informally monitored, and when repairs are called for, they are made. This is sometimes not the case in the centrally planned projects that remain alien to the local people and are under-utilized. Maintenance is rarely provided for completed projects, and they are abandoned after construction. When the construction is of questionable quality, due to the substitution of poorer materials, decay can be rapid, especially under extreme weather conditions. The general lack of proper post-construction supervision and maintenance has become a major issue.

Overall, the statistics of development have been inflated. Inappropriate constructions have been made with limited economic viability, often in the wrong places, under-utilized by a populace who do not understand their intent, and subject to rapid decay as a result of the combination of poor materials, inclement weather, and the lack of maintenance facilities.

*Local Attitudes Towards Aid Donors*

With a national debt of a little over 900 million US dollar which is 32.5 per cent of GNP (World Development Report,

1989) Nepal is yet one of the less indebted countries in the world. The net per capita disbursement of all foreign assistance, however, has been only 19.6 dollars(ibid). The absolute size of this national debt, however, may obscure the importance of foreign aid for to the national well-being. Nepal is currently dependent on foreign aid. Its total national expenditure is shown as 18.3 per cent of the GNP against 8.6 per cent of its revenue for the year 1987, which only means that its foreign dependence is constantly increasing over the years. The danger is that this dependence will become institutionalized. Current fatalistic beliefs would support such an institutionalization. The purpose of foreign aid is to develop a strong infrastructure that can generate its own process of growth, to address the economic needs of the people and raise the standard of living. Once the infrastructure is in place, and the initial capital investment has been made, the ideal expectation is to wean itself from its aid dependency. Nepal's success will then depend on the economic skills of her own people.

In past ages, indigenous skills served Nepal well, and Nepal was known for both its mercantilism and the sophistication of its technology. In the meantime certain qualities of the Nepali people have changed. Today, we are faced with the increasing prevalence of unethical behaviour with its central fatalistic beliefs. Such beliefs have permeated all levels of society. Fatalism is connected to dependency, robbing the people of personal control, and the sense of individual competence, their willingness to assume responsibility, thereby diminishing their motivation for personal achievement. It undermines the possibility of instrumental social action, without which economic success cannot be realized. It substitutes instead the perception that power and responsibility are qualities invested only in powerful others and, in the case of Nepal's dependence on foreign aid, those powerful others are the foreign aid donors. The ready provision of foreign aid, for those who are fatalistic, merely emulates an expected pattern. It reinforces a sense that Nepal is basically a weak and helpless country, while others are powerful yet beneficent. As the powerful appear to be so willing to provide economic nurturance, there then develops the view that there is both no need to change this new relationship, and that, even if there was a need, it would not be possible. The danger is that the relative poverty of Nepal will become institutionalized, and that its people will not be able to imagine anything other than that. Such an image will only act to dissipate any motivation for self-improvement.

The threat is not simply of economic dependency but of a form of ingrained social and psychological dependency as well. There increases the danger of developing a syndrome of being 'a poor nation', so that it becomes a matter of fact for people; cultivating a sense of pride and confidence in themselves becomes an extremely difficult task for the majority of people at any level. There is a Nepali proverb that describes the dangers of this situation : *choro maryo bhanera pir nagarnu; tara kal palkyo bhanera hos garnur ( do not feel too sorry for the death of one son but watch out that death might return again frequently).*

That so much wealth is entering the country in the form of foreign aid, and not as part of an exchange of Nepali productivity, has produced other problems. In particular, such massive foreign aid has helped mask widespread economic abuse and corruption. Such corruption has met with little opposition because almost all resources are beginning to come from the fortuitous sources of foreign aid. Through foreign aid, people are being provided with additional facilities such as schools, hospitals, roads, drinking water, and electricity. With such an improvement in their lot, there is little that the common people have to complain about. But opportunities are provided for others to become rich through the misuse of public money, and some appear to be doing it with impunity. For Nepali social observers, then, foreign aid has become particularly associated with corruption and what is seen as a new avenue for the exploitation of the people.

Critics have been quick to point this out and to utilize it in their attack on the establishment. Certain Nepali scholars have divided Nepali society into two distinct classes, namely the upper class and 'under class', and they complain that the first and very obvious political role of foreign aid consists in its overall support of the traditional power structure for the benefit, by definition, of the upper class (Mishra and Sharma, 1983). What these critics fail to appreciate, however, is that it is not principally the presence of foreign aid that is corrupting, but of fatalism and ascriptive values. These perpetuate passive dependence and, therefore, the vulnerability of the people along with a readiness to accept their lot as having been decreed by fate, and the expectation that people of a certain status have a prior claim to material benefits.

With increasing Nepali dependency on foreign aid, and the transference of much of the responsibility formally and otherwise, for its administration to the donors themselves, any criticism of the distribution of benefits, or impatience with the pace of development, all get blamed on these powerful external benefactors. Women are unhappy because foreign aid has not understood their problems (Pradhan and Shrestha, 1983). Agricultural economists complain that in spite of a massive amount of foreign investment, gains in productivity have not been spectacular (Pant, 1983). Foreign aid donors get blamed for not bringing bumper crops, industrial growth, and the much needed social reforms to the country.

Particularly irksome to the educated critics in Kathmandu has been the issue of salaries to foreign advisers. There are many Nepalis who rightly think that there are quite a few foreign experts who are earning ten times the salary of a Nepali with one-tenth of the skills or knowledge about the problem or the job (Shrestha:1983). Shrestha argues that foreign experts and advisers are overpaid, more than thirty to fifty times their counterparts in the Nepali government. He also believes in the comment of a UN expert that Nepal is 'over-advised and under-nourished'. The ethnocentrism of foreign developmental advisors has been reflected, not only in certain basic shortcomings in their perspectives on developmental problems, but in their regard for and interaction with their Nepali colleagues, who have sometimes felt slighted. Many Nepalis are now highly educated and possess critical technical skills and have a better understanding of the problems and needs of Nepal. Their difficulty, I believe, lies in their being enmeshed in the legacy of the hierarchic caste attitudes, no matter whether they themselves are overtly and consciously hierarchic or not. This situation makes the foreign adviser more effective than the local expert, even if he has the same skills but less knowledge of the situation. The local expert becomes quickly lost in fatalism and the intrigues associated with chakari and afno manchhe.

Echoing certain points that I have made here, the most noted critic of foreign aid, and a former member of the National Planning Commission observed that:

> The transplantation of foreign aid in a country without a social structure that is conducive to development can result in a cancerous type of growth... The problem is that only a few countries among the bilateral donors to Nepal have contributed aid in a manner that can lead to self-sustained growth... Foreign aid usually helps produce generalists who attend seminars but who do not work in the fields (Lohani, 1983).

While there are points of similarity, the difference is that my argument indicates fatalistic values as the root cause of the problem, while Lohani is pointing to powerful external others as the root source. This external projection, however, is merely consistent with the fatalistic world-view, in which he seems to be unwittingly caught. Lohani also argues that 'rural development requires political management, not foreign technical inputs...Technological inputs such as the rural transport system makes inroads for colonialism and comparable bourgeois systems' (ibid). This kind of criticism, in particular, seems to be connected with modern forms of seminar punditry, where secular erudition has been substituted for Vedic ritualistic erudition. These observations are not grounded in the realities of Nepali society. The vicissitudes of Nepali culture is what has been consistently ignored by foreign developmentalists and native critics.

It is not that difficult to see that the affluence and power achieved by the western European Christian society was not a geographical accident nor was the colonization of the Asian subcontinent primarily made possible by the greater firepower of the colonizers. It is the difference in value systems and lifestyles of the people that made it possible. Japanese economic and industrial power is the result of their value system that emphasizes on rational thinking, stimulates the desire for achievement, and which rewards hard work. A social observer from South Korea, a country which made rapid and dramatic progress in modernization during the past few decades, summed up the problem when he said:

> Problematic are social conditions in which one cannot work even if he wants to and a social structure under which, however hard he may work, one cannot succeed. An ideal society will allow men to work hard and guarantee success to hard-working men. A developing and healthy society should motivate men to engage in diligent labor and reward hard work accordingly (Rhee Kyu Ho, 1983).

Our current value system, at least that which dominates those critical sectors of society acting as mediators of foreign influence, has been subverted by the fatalistic elements of the caste system and this fatalism has had far-reaching consequences in all areas of society. The consequence of fatalism is debilitating to social advancement, and facilitates the abuse of the current transitional developmental process. Nepal cannot look to the cornucopia of foreign aid for solutions to all its problems and it is no use blaming it for the negative fallout of fatalistic beliefs.

Nepal is not alone in remaining backward and poor. There are many societies in the third world which are poor and backward. The reasons behind their backwardness are many and different though the symptoms are the same. Mostly, however, such societies discourage innovation. They tend to maintain themselves by fairly rigid prescriptions of fixed adult roles, into which both men and women are fitted. These expected social roles define the limits of aspiration for each generation. People who have made comparative studies of many different societies, know that when status is ascribed, rather than achieved, individual efforts towards excellence are not directed through any form of innovation; rather, the enhancement of status occurs only through the realization of a previously well defined role position. It is only with social change, or when some form of continual dynamic disequilibrium occurs in a society, that we begin to observe the development of achievement motivation in its modern form (De Vos, 1973).

Nepal will need foreign aid for quite some time to come, at least until it is able to develop an industrial base. Foreign aid has become an integral part of national economic and international political life. It would be short sighted to wish it away. There is no wisdom in blaming foreign aid and wishing for its discontinuation. This does not, however, mean that Nepal should wait for foreign aid to take care of all its needs while Nepalis sit back doing nothing themselves. The people have to work hard to help develop a higher standard of living.

The world has 'shrunk' because of the technological advancement of recent decades. Nepal cannot remain in isolation, but will, of necessity, be forced to become part of the world community. This cannot be otherwise, even if Nepal makes a conscious decision to remain poor and underdeveloped. Another observation from Rhee is of relevance to us here:

> The history of mankind is sometimes compared to a great symphony. All the nations, large and small, which have their own cultures are taking part in the symphony, each with its own unique sound. When some instruments make a false sound, the harmony will be weakened or finally destroyed. When the sound of strong instruments absorbs that of others, the symphony exhibits dissonance and the sound becomes cacophonous. To perform the symphony all nations must participate in the open interchange of cultures, each playing its own instrument (Rhee, 1983).

Foreign aid can facilitate Nepal becoming a fully functioning and productive member of this community. But it needs to be used realistically and beneficially, and this can only be done when it is spent on training the common people who will use these skills, rather than educating aspiring individuals with hierarchic attitude to become pedagogues to preach pessimism and infuse a very poor self-image as they themselves have had for a long time. The Nepali population that has remained untouched by Hindu caste principles is Nepal's greatest treasure. This is a very sizable proportion of the population. But presently they live in remote areas, at a little above subsistence level, with little or no education, and no opportuities to develop and actualize their aspirations. Their values are not the values of hierarchic Bahunism. They do know the importance of hard work, of endurance, and the role of individual effort in the improvement of ones' circumstances. And they have the positive qualities of strong cooperative behavior and an appreciation of the general well being and importance of the group or community as a whole. The Jyapu in Kathmandu Valley, and the others who are even less affected by Hindu caste hierarchy, such as the Sherpa, Tamang, Magar and Limbus are untapped resources of the nation. Only when foreign aid can reach these people, in sufficient quantity and of the right kind, will Nepal genuinely be able to establish the basis of her future prosperity.

## NOTES AND REFERENCES

1 The planned target by the turn of the century is to host more than one million tourists a year.
2 He used money from the Pashupatinath Trust for the reconstruction of Kathmandu instead.
3 Progress Report of the First Five Year Plan: Nepal National Planning Council.

# CONCLUSION

In Nepal, government statistics are available on critical aspects of the economy, but little exists by way of social statistics. There are estimations of total population, and some attempt is made to index changes in the birth rate. Significantly, figures for the populations of the various ethnic groups do not exist. We do not know what the relative incidence of Khas and Kirat groups are within the population; we do not know how many Gurungs, Magars, Limbus, Jirels, or Tharus there really are. This ignorance is used to support a major distortion in the characterization of the Nepali people. Without any real information to the contrary, the tendency within the administration is to perceive Nepal as a country with a predominantly homogenous religious and cultural pattern. This is a misrepresentation. High caste Hindus have been portrayed as the majority of the population, with the Matwali being considered a minority. It is considered only natural that the culture of majority group becomes the legitimate national culture, and that the hierarchization of the ethnic peoples is continuous with the development of a consolidated national identity.

In part, such a misconstruction results from a tendency to perceive the caste system as an inevitable condition for a legitimate Hindu kingdom and as being coextensive with the use of Nepali as a first language. But Nepali, originally the language of the Khas in the west, was adopted by many Tibeto-Burmese speaking peoples in the Khas Empire and became increasingly important within the Kathmandu Valley before unification[1]. Unification, to a large extent, merely formalized what was already happening, but did extend the Nepali language further into the east. Many Kirat people hence speak Nepali. Further, many of the Gurungs, Magars, Tharus and Khas are Matwali and are not treated as high caste. Khas people are Matwali except those who have Chhetrized themselves by wearing the ritual thread. The Bahun-Chhetri, then are in a minority.

Though a minority they are a powerful one. A vast majority of teachers, university professors, academicians, intellectuals and journalists are the high caste Hindus, namely the Bahun-Chhetri, and the Shresthas among Newars, who are equally hierarchic in their overall attitude towards the rest of the Nepali people. Consequently, the derivation and transmission of information about Nepal, and about the outside world, takes place through the hands of these people who are highly hierarchic in their attitude. A result of this hierarchism is a tendency to disparage things Nepali, depreciating national accomplishments while exalting those of India and the plains, the birthplace of caste Hinduism. The true base of the Nepali social order are sought to be located by them within Indian Brahmanic historical traditions. A fatalistic orientation also contributes to a sense of passivity and defeatism towards the prospects for a revitalization of Nepali society. Key elements of the Indian influence, then, are the depreciation of things Nepali, Indianization of religious culture, poor self image and fatalistic resignation. Through their control of information dissemination and education, these sentiments become broadly dispersed.

High caste Hindus and others who have been influenced by it are strongly represented in government administration. The civil service plays a considerable role in the political life of the country and, over the past thirty years, has been the effective body of government. Outside the priesthood, which is an exclusive privilege of the Bahuns, an occupation within the administrative bureaucracy is a traditional avenue of employment for the high caste i.e., Bahun-Chhetri and Shrestha who, with the right afno manchhe connections, could expect a speedy placement regardless of actual need within the bureaucracy. Many of these high caste people regard such a placement as their natural right. The Nepali civil service, then, has a tendency to expand, not in response to an increase in organizational functions or productive need, but as a response to an increase in its popularity among the upper caste people as a source of employment. The organizational form of the bureaucracy reflects the vicissitudes of chakari. Bureaucratic practices have been strongly influenced by caste-class attitudes, and decisions made within the bureaucracy are strongly guided, if not determined, by fatalistic sentiment. Because foreign aid operates through the civil service, fatalistic people have acted as key intermediaries between the provision of these external resources and their eventual allocation. More generally, they have acted to mediate most relations between Nepal and the outside world. This has directly influenced development in Nepal in all dimensions.

The upper castes are strongly represented in politics.[2] They have been most successful in the political arena, with a different political agenda and style of campaign. Many among them are isolated from the people, with an abrupt and elusive interpersonal style, and tend to base their campaigns on abstract issues. Only a few among them are approachable, interact with the people, and address concrete issues that an electorate can appreciate. But many remain persistent outsiders and their isolation and alienation sometimes results in the cultivation of revolutionary sympathies. Rather than being a part of the established though developing political apparatus, such individuals feed the ranks of the revolutionaries and idealistic democrats — both of whom espouse abstract utopian philosophies, having little contact with the genuine needs of the people and their culture. Such people, then, become key elements of political opposition.

The extremely hierarchized individuals appear to be having the hardest time in adjusting to change. Many seem to be caught with the expectation of being automatically provided for. They are perhaps the most dependent of all Nepalis, but the society that supported them in the past does not do so today, and many have not adapted to it. It is among the highest castes that one finds the strongest indications of anomie consequent on the processes of acculturation. Ironically, though the caste-related designation of Matwali, meaning alcohol drinking, is applied to the lower caste and ethnic groups, it is among the thread-wearing high caste that serious alcoholism currently appears to be growing.

While not all high caste Hindus are orthodox, even the irreligious ones can remain the victims of their hierarchic upbringing and be greatly affected by fatalistic beliefs. Some, as a result of their personal experiences and reflections, develop a strong opposition towards fatalism itself but replace it with something that at an abstract level has remarkable similarities to many of the features of caste hierarchy, and they continue to behave as pundits. They may be atheistic, international travellers with an education abroad, having professional degrees, but their orientation to development and their way of action remains influenced by caste principles. They are passive defeatists, who see an impoverished Nepal and lose any hope for the future (see Khanal,1987). Many are embarassed by things Nepali, which they think are inferior, and they look to the outside world as the source for sophistication and cultivation. They intellectualize problems and subject them to endless debate, while passing on any real responsibility for decision making to some higher level. Their new, superfical, membership to the world culture becomes an opportunity for self-distinction from the uneducated and unsophisticated common mass. They make use of chakari and, when in privileged positions, with their perception that the country cannot be greatly helped, use the opportunity to help themselves and their afno manchhe.

Not all educated people are from a high caste background, but even an aspiring non-caste ethnic individual, who has succeeded through personal effort to gain an education and a respected position, when acculturated with the caste people develops hierarchic caste attitudes. This is the great current danger of a Hindu high caste dominated value system: that it is readily secularized and can be recreated anew by those not traditionally of the caste background. But Nepal is passing through a stage of transition, and traditional social structures are being modified to accommodate change, with ever newer social organizations being introduced. For some, this is a time of opportunity, though the opportunity should be for all. In this time of flux it has become apparent that the adverse features of Bahunism can be promulgated and perpetuated by members of any social class or ethnic group. With a history of caste, there is a danger of the development of a new secularized caste system, where the socially mobile consolidate their position by blocking out their competitors or those closely behind them.

The high caste people are in a minority, and their value system is not the prevalent value system among the majority of the people in Nepal. Yet fatalism and hierarchy, the hallmarks of the caste principles, must be taken very seriously and must be recognized as the most influential value system. Any strategy for development, if it is to be genuine, and not a redistribution of foreign monies into local hands, must oppose fatalism and a hierarchic social order, because the two are irreconcilable. This need not be traumatic for Nepal, because the form of fatalism associated with the caste hierarchy is not Nepali even though it is sometimes believed to be so by some people. Nepal has other value systems to draw upon, that have much greater potential. These are the value systems of the traditional ethnic groups of the country who are not divided into a vertical hierarchic order and are as a rule hard-working with a conscientious discipline.They also share a sense of guilt within their own context, which the fatalistic people have lost altogetherwith the introduction of the ritual of giving charity to a priest to absolve a sense of guilt.

Like many other ethnic peoples the Jyapu peasants and other professional groups among the Newars still have much to offer. They are the craftsmen and other skilled workers who are the descendents of those responsible for the great days of Kathmandu's past. The creativity of these people has been intermittently suppressed, but under the right circumstances has readily blossomed. For a thousand years, in the time of the Licchavis, they supported the kingdom, and during the breakup of the medieval period, when circumstances favoured, they again displayed their excellence. If they feel socially oppressed or disparaged, and if their work is taken with little in exchange, it is not likely that any creativity and industry will be forthcoming. But with encouragement and opportunity their values and ideals represent a great, and presently unappreciated, resource. They have a commitment to work. What they need is a stimulation of their motivation, and this can happen when the general lethargy of society, consequent to fatalism, has been discarded.

Outside the Kathmandu Valley, there are the various ethnic peoples of Nepal, who remain uncounted, and underconsidered. Their culture is regarded as primitive and of no importance. This is a grave error. As mentioned in the first chapter, the various ethnic peoples are of two main stock groups, the Indo-Aryan Khas and the Tibeto-Burmese Kirat, with some suggestions of Dravidian admixtures in the south.

Culturally, there is also a range, with a few hunters and gatherers and pastoralists, the bulk being agriculturalists. Others, mainly the highland dwellers such as the Sherpa, Manange, and Thakali, are strongly mercantile.

Though these various ethnic groups differ from one another in many details, for the most part they share significant values and social institutions in common. The peasants inhabit a village society. The village is a relatively discrete unit, with a known geographic boundary. There is an intimacy between the people of the village and the land they live on and cultivate. The intimacy is based on the people's dependency on the land for nurturance, which requires that they be particularly sensitive to its perturbations and the methods by which it might be revitalized. To ensure their continued nurturance in this manner, the people have over a long period of time developed particular practical technologies, the application of which helps to ensure the productivity of the land. Supplementing these agricultural technologies is the development of systems of magical and spiritual control of the local forces of nature: through worship, appeasement in sacrifice, or various kinds of cajolery. Meanwhile, there has developed a sense of debt and awe to the ancestors who were responsible for the development of this harmonious society. A widespread practice in Nepal is for people to believe that the ancestors of each clan coalesce into a single spiritual entity, which is the clan deity. Clan deities are often merged with the deities of nature. Consequently, there is a complete unity in the relations between things, both human and natural. This could help not only to increase productivity but also to improve environment and nature conservation.

The village is inhabited by familiar people, with known abilities and predispositions. As there is a dependence of the people as a whole on the land, so there is an inter-dependence among the people, to cooperate in the management of that land, forest, and water and in harvesting its products. The village is an efficiently productive and harmonious social group. Within it, the individual develops a sense of self which is embedded in a particular social network that has continuity. In many cases that continuity is grounded in the connection to the common clan deity, with which all social actors within the clan will eventually merge. The sense of self is not a separated one, individually empowered to take personal responsibility and control over the individual's actions. The self is connected to the group in a way that appears to be common to, and has been studied more thoroughly, if not definitively, in East Asia, and it is not the same with the earlier mentioned phenomenon of afno manchhe.

In East Asian societies, some have talked of a collectivistic self, as opposed to an individualistic found in Western societies. This particular construction of self, common in Nepal, is very capable of productive and creative effort, and its potential for success is demonstrated in the success of the Japanese, Koreans, and the Chinese in Taiwan and Singapore. In Japan, in particular, the economic-business applications of the social organization built upon such group-self definition are clearly a main ingredient of the success, attributed by some to Japanese management — to some not attentive to it, it is an elusive quality that they have tried to theoretically isolate and replicate in inappropriate cultural environments, such as in American attempts at importing Japanese management practices. This potential for the strong commitment of the self to the group and the benefits of cooperative action can be very vital factors in the successful development of Nepal's inner potential.

Of course the Japanese tendency to collectivism is not identical with that of Nepal's, and may be stronger, reinforced by a series of other factors that are not shared in Nepal. There is the important question of motivation. Japanese men, in particular, have been characterized as being impelled by a strong sense of filial obligations, especially towards the mother (Doi 1962), and this sense of obligation has become internalized as a strong but productive sense of guilt (De Vos, 1973). High caste Hindu Nepalis do not have such a sense of guilt, so that the motivation will have to come from elsewhere. This could be developed with further research on causes of motivation among the working people at different levels.

Other qualities discovered in the Japanese as contributing to their success are their capacities for hard work and for endurance, including the developed expectation that nothing comes easily and that goals may not even be realized for several generations (De Vos, op cit). Both of these qualities are very evident among the ethnic peoples of Nepal. While aesthetically beautiful, the geography of Nepal for the most part is not easy to live with. Its harshness plays a big role in the development of endurance among the Nepalis. In most areas, only the hardest of work ensures survival of self, family and community. There has developed among the Nepali people, then, many of the very qualities found to be critical to Japanese success.

The Thakali people of the Gandaki region have been working, as an entire group, for several generations to transform their wealth and status (Bista,1971). The name Thakali, according to them, is a recent adoption, and is a corruption of Thakuri — an index of their intentions, as well as pretensions. The irony of the situation is that they want to change their caste and not remain Matwali. Within the Nepali caste system, this is a possibility. The economic base of their hopes is mercantile. They had established themselves in critical positions on what had the potential to be a major trade route out of the Tibetan plateau, and then developed the means to best exploit that position. But with the increasing interest in raising their status to the level of the Thakuri, many among them have been attracted towards the fatalistic hierarchy, just like the feudalistic Khas of the Karnali basin and the bourgeoisie among the Newars of Kathmandu Valley had been a few centuries earlier (ibid).

Mercantile activity has been successfully practised by the ethnic people of Nepal since the earliest days. Proto-historical records first mention the peoples of Nepal in connection with trade goods, originating in the high Tibetan plateau. It was only afterwards that the people of Nepal became famous for their own industry. But under fatalistic caste principles imported from India, mercantile activity was disparaged as a polluting activity. Not only is it a form of labour, but it is crassly materialistic. Merchants were thus considered low caste. Much as what happened in China under Confucianism, the people's natural inclination towards and dexterity in mercantile trades was greatly dampened. Where the Chinese people have moved away from the strictures of traditional Confucianist society, such as in the overseas communities, this natural flair for mercantile activity has been rekindled with spectacular results. Such could be the case with the Nepali people as well, once freed from the negative aspects of the ascriptive caste values and fatalism.

Among the ethnic peoples, then, there are located some very significant human and cultural resources. These people are hard working, persevering and long suffering, cooperate well and work with a dedication towards collective well-being, and have the qualities needed to be successful merchants. But rather than being tapped, these resources are being shunted aside, ignored, and worse, destroyed, to be replaced with the qualities of punditry — abhorrence of work, hierarchism and the willingness to exploit others, passive dependence, and fatalism. For example, the widely publicised mass Vratabandha ceremonys have negative effects of hierarchization and destruction on the egalitarian base of the Nepali society at large.

One of the main arguments put forward for the elimination of the various ethnic cultures is the need to develop a strong national identity. Some pundits are arguing that this can only be possible with cultural homogeneity — with the complete institution of caste values. But pluralism is not necessarily a problem for the development of some larger encompassing social entity, such as a nation. Ethnic pluralism, to some degree, is a reality in nearly all societies. It is not pluralism, per se, that acts against the formation of nationhood, though the nature of relations between the various groups may act to do so. In this case, the upper caste-class people must realize that they are merely one of the elements within this pluralism. They too are an ethnic minority. They should not insist on the imposition of the values of one minority over the others as a solution, especially where the values are manifested in a social hierarchy with themselves at the top and the others beneath them.

The others have resisted this solution for two thousand years. This is the only way they could maintain their dignity and self respect. Nepali people's self respect and dignity cannot be maintained when the small number of upper caste-class people consistently treat the majority as lower in the hierarchic order. The only product of this was resentment, a retreat away from national into ethnic identity, and a sense of resentment and even hostility to the state. This in fact is a very well known phenomenon the world over. Minority people struggle for an identity, and demand that the identity be publicly acknowledged as having import. They also demand progress, a rising standard of living, effective political order wherein they have their own role recognised properly, and greater social justice (Geertz 1973).

The solution of the hierarchic upper caste people of national identity is effectively to impede it. Imposition of a fatalistic hierarchic caste tradition is not a solution to the desire for nationalism. Sadly, the far-sighted advice of the great king Prithvi Narayan Shah, to treat Nepal as the garden of four castes and thirty-six ethnic communities, was ignored. For his coronation, he would have been happy to have been anointed by the priests of all ethnic groups, such as Limbu, Rai, Tamang, Gurung, Tharu and Dhimal instead of subjugating them under a narrow hierarchic caste structure.

To be acceptable to all, the nation must rise above the interests of any one specific group. It must encompass all their aspirations and be the vehicle and support for their transformation into successfully adapted modern societies. Their neglect will support future problems, because the process of transformation is not an easy one, nor does it have a natural predetermined course. There are many dangers of negative side-effects of acculturation, and the later these are recognized as a problem, the greater they will be and the more difficult it will be to provide satisfying solutions. Social mistakes can become institutionalized, and the Nepalis of future generations will have to live with them as part of their inheritance. The earlier the issues of ethnicity are recognized, the better it will be, provided they are dealt with studiously and objectively.

The King is a positive force for the country and an active catalyst for the process of nationhood because all Nepalis share a tendency for paternal dependency, which, in social organization, faciliates a kind of perspective that monarchy provides an ultimate beneficent paternal figure. This is both reassuring to the Nepali, and also becomes the basis of his developing sense of national identity. The nation includes all those that enjoy the munificence of this common father. It is an extension of family, of village, of clan, of ethnic group, that brings a new completion by incorporating all surrounding ethnic groups into a common fold. This is inherently good, because it acts to harmonize relations between groups. But recognizing any single cultural group as important and ignoring others can be unwise as it helps instill a sense of insecurity among those who are treated with less importance.

The campaign of thread-wearing Vratabandha ceremony which is being popularized by some high caste people had had its own justification to have royal patronage during the medieval period. But today it is in the style of treating everyone as equal that we have a chance in helping the process of national integretion. An effective political system cannot afford to allow itself to be dominated by a privileged group nor can its leaders afford to allow themselves to be manipulated by unprincipled chakari practitioners. Competence and integrity even when not accompanied by finesse and style deserves strong support at this stage in our history when economic development and national integration are by far the most important priorities.

As Nepal changes, as the different ethnic societies change, much of indigenous culture will be modified or abandoned. Vacuums will be created, along with anxieties. The thrust of traditional culture has been towards the development and maintenance of cohesion and harmony, and one of the basic tools to ensure this in any society is stability and certainty. Nepal must now learn to live with change and uncertainty. Social health can only be ensured by flexibility. The very simplicity of most of the ethnic cultures allows a greater flexibility than does the cumbersome and ossified structure of urbane upper caste-class society in the Kathmandu valley. Nepal's future hopes lie with them. But they are a fragile resource as well, and need support and direction from some dependable source. Nepali youths have to be encouraged to ask questions about the future direction of society. Confidence in themselves and pride in the nation, currently crippled by fatalism, will have to be carefully cultivated. It is difficult but not impossible as there are quite a few examples in the history of the world around us. It may even be painful but has become an absolute necessity. A paragraph by Hermann Hesse quoted by William Ophuls from *Steppenwolf* might be appropriately repeated here:

> Every age, every culture, every custom and tradition has its own character, its own weakness and its own strengths, its beauties and ugliness; accepts certain suf-

ferings as matters of course, puts up patiently with certain evils. Human life is reduced to real suffering, to hell, only when two ages, two cultures and religions overlap.... Now there are times when a whole generation is caught in this way between two ages, two modes of life, with the consequence that it loses all power to understand itself and has no standard, no security, no simple aquiescence'.

The only way out of the suffering of the transition is to construct the new age as rapidly as possible, so that we are no longer caught between two ages (Ophuls, 1977). I really wonder whether any thoughtful, honest and future oriented sensible person will believe, for a moment, that the 'new age' is the age of fatalistic hierarchism, even though it was nurtured carefully and passionately for a couple of centuries, eloquently and rhetorically justified by some learned but fatalistic Pundits and legally endorsed by an authoritarian regime during the middle of the nineteenth century for its own selfish interest. We are working today for the well being of the future generations and not for the revival of the archaic values of hierarchic caste discipline evolved by the ancient Hindu society of India. Nor are we working to help the future generations carry the self-image of the poorest and the most backward people in the hierarchy of the world economic order.

NOTES AND REFERENCES

1 Even after a large number of the former Tibeto-Burmese speaking ethnic people began to speak Nepali as their mother tongue the total percentage of the Nepali speakers was 51%. The remaining 49% were recorded to be speaking various mother tongues other than Nepali in the census report of 1961 (see Bista 1972)

2. Of all the people who have been members of the National Panchayat since 1963 through 1988, 380 out of the total of 501,seventysix per cent have been from the high caste groups e.g., Bahun, Chhetri, Thakuri, Rajput Shrestha and Yadav.

# BIBLIOGRAPHY

Acharya Baburam. 1952. 'Nepal, Newar ra Newari Bhasa' (Nepal, Newar and Newari Language). *Nepal Sanskritic Parishad Patrika*. 1: 1-16.

—— . 1970. 'Nepalma Jalasayan Narayan Murtiko Sthapana' (Installation of a statue of Jalasayan Narayan). *Nepali*. 45: 3-24.

His Majesty's Press Secretariat. 1967. *Sri Panch Bada Maharajdhiraj, Prithvinarayan Shahko Sanchhipta Jivani* (Short Biography of King Prithvinarayan Shah). 4 Vols. Kathmandu.

Acharya, Laxmi. 1986. 'Kiratle Pani Janai Lae' (Even Kirats wore the sacred thread). *Kirateswor Sandesh* (Mahaprabhu Falgunanda Memorial Volume). 2: 30-33.

Acharya, Meena. 1981. 'The Maithili Women of Sirisa: The status of women in Nepal'. Kathmandu: CEDA, Tribhuvan University.

Adhikari, Surya Mani. 1988. *The Khas Kingdom: A Trans Himalayan Empire of the Middle Ages*. Jaipur: Nivala Publications.

Allen, N. J. 1981. 'The Thulung Myth of Bhume Sites and Some Indo-Tibetan Comparisons' in *Asian Highland Societies*, edited by C. V. Furer-Haimendorf. New Delhi: Sterling.

Allen, Michael. 1973. 'Buddhism without Monks: The Vajrayana Religion of the Newars of Kathmandu Valley'. *Journal of South Asia Studies*. 3: 1-14.

—— . 1982. 'Girls' Pre-puberty Rites Among the Newars of Kathmandu Valley' in *Women in India and Nepal*, edited by M. Allen and S. N. Mukherjee. *A. N. U. Monographs on South Asia*. Volume 8.

Aziz, Barbara N. 1978. *Tibetan Frontier Families*. New Delhi: Vikas Publishing House.

Ballinger, Thomas O. 1973. 'Simaraungarh Revisited: A Report on Some Observations Made at the Ruins of the Former Capital of Mithila in the Terai of Nepal'. *Kailash*. Volume 1, number 3, 180-84.

Banerjee, N. R. 1966. 'An Introduction to Nepalese Art'. *Nepalese Art*. 13-36. Kathmandu: Department of Archaelogy, HMGN.

Banerjee, N. R. and Sharma, Janak Lal. 1969. 'Neolithic Tools from Nepal and Sikkim'. *Ancient Nepal*. 9: 53-58.

Bangdal, Lain Singh. 1982. *Prachin Nepali Murtikalako Itihas*. Kathmandu: Royal Nepal Academy.

___ . 1982. *The Early Scriptures of Nepal*. New Delhi: Vikas Publishing House.

Banskota, Mahesh. 1983. 'Foreign Aid and the Poor: Some Observations on Nepal's Experience', in *Foreign Aid and Development in Nepal: Proceedings of a Seminar*. Kathmandu: IDS.

Baral, Lok Raj. 1977. *Oppositional Politics in Nepal*. New Delhi: Abhinav Publications.

Benedict, Ruth. 1946. *The Crysanthemum and the Sword: Patterns of Japanese Culture*. New York: Meridian Books.

Bennett, Lynn. 1978. 'Sitting in a Cave: An Analysis of Ritual Seclusion at Menarche among Brahmans and Chhetris in Nepal'. *Contributions to Nepalese Studies*. Volume 6, number 1, 31-46.

___ . 1983. *Dangerous Wives and Sacred Sisters: Social and Symbolic Roles of High Caste Women in Nepal*. New York: Columbia University Press.

Berreman, Gerald. 1964. 'Brahmans and Shamans in Pahari Religion' in *South Asia*, edited by Edwards B. Harpels. Seattle: University of Washington Press.

___ . 1972. *Hindus of the Himalayas: Ethnography and Change.* Berkeley: University of California Press.

Betteille, A. 1967. 'Elite Status Groups and Caste in Modern India' in *India and Ceylon: Unity and Diversity,* edited by P. Mason. London: Oxford University Press.

___ . 1984. *Individualism and the Persistence of Collective Identities.* Colchester: University of Sussex.

___ . 1985. *Equality of Opportunity and the Equal distribution of Benefits.* Kale Memorial Lecture. Pune: Gokhale Institute of Politics and Economics.

Bhasin, A. S., ed. 1970. *Documents on Nepal's Relations with India and China, 1949-66.* Bombay: Academic Books Limited.

Bista, Dor Bahadur. 1967. *People of Nepal.* Kathmandu: Department of Information and Broadcasting, HMGN. (5th edn. Kathmandu: Ratna Pustak Bhandar.)

___ . 1970. 'Social Aspects of a Hindu Kingdom' in *Nepal: A Profile,* edited by B. P. Shrestha. Kathmandu: Economic Research Council.

___ . 1971. 'The Political Innovators of Upper Kaligandaki'. *MAN.* 6: 52-60.

___ . 1976. 'Encounter with the Raute: Last Hunting Nomads of Nepal'. *Kailash.* 4: 317-27.

___ . 1977. 'Rastriya Ekikaran' in *Ruprekha* (Special issue), edited by Uttam Kunwar. Kathmandu: Rupayan Prakashan.

___ . 1977. 'Nepalis in Tibet' in *Himalayan Anthropology: The Indo Tibetan Interface,* edited by James Fischer, The Hague: Mouton.

___ . 1982. 'The Process of Nepalization'. *Anthropological and Linguistic Studies of the Gandaki Area in Nepal.* Tokyo: Institute for the Study of Languages and Cultures of Asia and Africa, Tokyo University of Foreign Studies.

___ . 1989a. 'Nepal in 1988'. *Asian Survey.* 29: 223-28.

——. 1989b. 'The Structure of Nepali Society' in *Nepal: Perspectives on Continuity and Change*, edited by Kamal P. Malla. Kathmandu: CNAS, Tribhuvan University.

Bista, Hikmat. 1976. 'A Nepalese Community Facing Changes and Development Problems' in *Himalaya Ecologie Ethnologie 268*. Paris: CNRS.

Bista, Keshar Bahadur. 1976. 'The Rastriya Vikas Seva: National Development Service' in *Himalaya Ecologie Ethnologie 268*. Paris: CNRS.

Bista, Khem Bahadur. 1972. *Le Culte du Kuldevta au Nepal, en particular chez certains Kshetri de le Vallee de Kathmandu*. Paris: CNRS.

Bista, Som Dhoj. 1982. *Nepal Garh* (Nepal Fort). Lalitpur: Kancharanjan Bista.

——. 1963. *Sahi Sainik Itihas* (History of the Royal Army). Kathmandu: Narayan Jung Shah.

Blaikie, P., Cameron, John and Seddon, David. 1980. *Nepal in Crisis, Growth and Stagnation at the Periphery*. Delhi: Oxford University Press.

Bouillier, Veronique. 1977. 'Economic Relationship between Occupational Castes and High Castes in Central Nepal'. *Contributions to Nepalese Studies*. 4: 99-110.

Burghart, Richard. 1978. 'The History of Janakpur'. *Kailash*. 6: 257-84.

——. 1983. 'For a Sociology of Indias: An Intracultural Approach to the Study of Hindu Society'. *Contributions to Indian Sociology*. London: Sage Publications.

——. 1984. 'The Formation of the Concept of Nation-State in Nepal'. *Journal of Asian Studies*. 44: 101-25.

Caplan, A. P. 1972. *Priests and Cobblers: A Study of Social Change in a Hindu Village in Western Nepal*. London: Intertext Books.

Caplan, L. 1970. *Land and Social Change in East Nepal*. London: Routledge and Kegan Paul.

____. 1971. 'Cash and Kind: Two Media of Bribery in Nepal'. *MAN*. 6: 266-78.

____. 1975. *Administration and Politics in a Nepalese Town*. London: Oxford University Press.

Chatterji, Bhola. 1967. *A Study of Recent Nepalese Politics*. Calcutta: World Press.

Chemjog, Iman Singh. 1966-67. *History and Culture of the Kirat People*. 2 vols. Nepal: Tumen Hang, Chandra Dev Hang.

Coburn, Broughton. 1982. *Nepali Aama: Poitrait of a Nepalese Hill Woman*. California: Ross Erickson Inc.

Dahal, D. R. 1983. 'Economic Development through Indigenous Means; A Case of Indian Migration in the Nepal Terai'. *Contributions to Nepalese Studies*. Volume 11, number 1: 1-20.

____. 1989. 'Population Growth, Land Pressure and Development of Cash Crops in a Nepali Village'. *Contributions to Nepalese Studies*. Volume 13, number 1: 1-10.

Dahal, D. R., Rai, N. K. and Manzardo, A. E. 1977. *Land and Migration in Far-Western Nepal*. Kathmandu: INAS, Tribhuvan University.

Devkota, Grishma Bahadur. 1959. *Nepalko Rajnaitik Darpan* (volume 1). Kathmandu: Keshav Chandra Gautam.

____. 1970. *Nepalko Rajnaitik Darpan* (volume 2). Kathmandu: Bhattarai Bandhu.

De Vos, George A. ed. 1973. *Socialization for Achievement: Essays on the Cultural Psychology of the Japanese*. Berkeley: UC Press.

Dhungel, Ramesh. 1986. *Nepalko Arthik Itihas: Prachin Artha Vyabastha* (Economic history of Nepal: ancient economy). Kathmandu: S. P. Upadhyaya Dhungel.

Doherty, Victor S. 1978. 'Notes on the Origins of the Newars of the Kathmandu Valley of Nepal' in *Himalayan Anthropology: The Indo Tibetan Interface*, edited by J. Fisher. The Hague: Mouton.

Doi, Takeo. 1962. '"Amae": A Key concept for understanding Japanese Personality Structure' in *Japanese Culture*, edited by R. J. Smith and R. K. Beardsley. Chicago: Aldine.

____ . 1971. *The Anatomy of Dependence.* Tokyo: Kodansha.

Edgerton, Franklin. trans. 1964. *The Bhagavad Gita.* New York: Harper and Row.

Elder, Joseph W. 1970. *Planned Resettlement in Nepal's Terai.* Kathmandu: INAS, Tribhuvan University.

Fisher, James F. 1978. 'Homo Hierarchicus Nepalensis: A Cultural Sub-species' in *Himalayan Anthropology: The Indo Tibetan Interface* edited by J. Fisher. The Hague: Mouton.

____ . 1986. *Transhimalayan Traders.* Berkeley: University of California Press.

Fried, Morton. 1960. 'On the Evolution of Social Stratification and the State' in *Culture in History: Essays in Honour of Paul Radin.* New York: Colombia University Press.

Furer-Haimendorf, C. von. 1962. 'Caste in the Multi-ethnic Society of Nepal'. *Contributions to Indian Sociology.* 6: 12-32.

____ . 1964. *The Sherpas of Nepal.* London: John Murray.

____ . 1975 *Himalayan Traders.* London. John Murray.

Gaborieau, Marc. 1966. 'Muslims in the Hindu Kingdom of Nepal'. *Contributions to Indian Sociology.* 6: 84-105.

____ . 1976. 'Preliminary Report on the God Mashta' in *Spirit Possession in the Nepal Himalayas.* New Delhi: Vikas Publishing House.

Gaige, Frederick, 1975. *Regionalism and National Unity in Nepal.* Berkeley: UC Press.

Gauchan, P. 1981. *'Hamro Desh, Hamro Jati': Nepalka Thakali Karuko ek Parichaya* (Our Land, Our People: An Introduction to the Thakalis of Nepal). Kathmandu: L. S. Gauchan.

Gauchan, S. and Vinding, Michael. 1977. 'History of the Thakali Tradition'. *Kailash*. Volume 5, number 2, 97-184.

Geertz, Clifford. 1973. *Interpretation of Cultures*. New York: Basic Books.

Gellner, David N. 1986. 'Language, Caste, Religion and Territory: Newar Identity, Ancient and Modern'. *European Journal of Sociology*.

Gnoli, G. 1984. 'Guiseppe Tucci 1894-1984' *East and West Roma*: ISMEO, volume 34, numbers 1-3.

Goldstein, Melvin. 1974. 'Population, Social Structure and Strategic Behaviour: An Essay on Polyandry, Fertility and Changes in Limi Panchayat'. *Contributions to Nepalese studies*. Volume 4, number 2, 21-42.

Gurung, Ganesh Man. 1984. *Dura Jaatko Samajik Adhyayan* (Study of Dura Society). Kathmandu: Gurung.

Grurung, Harka. 1979. *Vignettes of Nepal*. Kathmandu: Sajha Prakashan.

Gurung, Jag Man. 1984. *Nepalko Eki Karanma Gurungharuko Bhumika* (Role of Gurungs in the Unification of Nepal). Pokhara: Sri Banddha Arghau Sadan.

Gyawali, Surya Bikram, 1962. *Nepal Upatyakato Madhyakalin Itihas*. Kathmandu: Royal Nepal Academy.

Gyawali, Tirtha Prasad. 1977. *Magtanpurvaka Magtaharu*. Nepalganj: Panchayat Development Training Centre.

Hamilton, Francis B. *An Account of the Kingdom of Nepal and of the Territories Annexed to this Dominion by the House of the Gorkhas*. Edinburgh: Archibald Company.

Harris, Marvin. 1974. *Cows, Pigs, Wars and Witches*. New York: Random House.

Hitchcock, John T. and Jones, Rex L. eds. 1976. *Spirit Possession in the Nepal Himalayas*. Delhi: Vikas Publishing House.

Hodgeson, B. H. *Essays on the Languages, Literature and Religion of Nepal and Tibet*. London: Trubner & Company.

Hofer, Andres. 1979. *The Caste Hierarchy and the State in Nepal, A Study of the Mulki Ain of 1854*. Transbruck: Universitatsverlag Wagner.

____. 1979. 'On Re-reading le Nepal: What we Social Scientists owe to Sylvain Levi'. *Kailash*. Volume 7, numbers 3 and 4, 175-190.

Hogger, R. 1976. 'Cultural Systems and Ecological Crisis in Nepal: Towards better Co-operation between Anthropologists and Decision makers'. *Himalaya Ecologie Ethnologie 268*. 547-556. Paris: CNRS.

Holmberg, David, 1989. *Order in Paradox: Myth, Ritual and Exchange among Nepal's Tamang*. Ithaca, New York: Cornell University Press.

Iijima, Shigeru. 1977. 'Ecology, Economy and Cultural Change Among the Thakalis in the Himalayas of Central Nepal' in *Changing Aspects of Modern Nepal*. Tokyo: Institute for the Study of Languges and Cultures of Asia andAfrica, Tokyo University of Foreign Studies.

Ishii, Hiroshi. 1982. 'Agricultural Labour Recruitment in a Parbate Village in Nepal' in *Anthropological and Linguistic Studies of the Gandaki Area of Nepal*. Tokyo: Institute for the Study of Languages and Culture of Asia and Africa, Tokyo University of Foreign Studies.

Jackson, Anthony. ed. 1987. 'Anthropology at Home'. *ASA Monograph* 25. London: Tavistock Publications Limited.

Jackson, D. P. 1977. 'The Early History of Lo(Mustang) and Ngari'. *Contributions to Nepalese Studies*. Volume 4, number 1.

Jain, M. S. N. 1972. *The Emergence of a New Aristocracy in Nepal*. Agra: Sri Ram Mehra.

Jest, C. 1977. 'The Kuswar of Chaitali (Central Nepal)' *Contributions to Nepalese Studies*. Volume 4, number 2, 1-45.

Jones, Shirly Kurz and Jones, Rex-.1976. 'Limbu Women, Divorce and the Domestic Cycle'. *Kailash*. 4: 169-84.

Jones, Rex.L. 1976. 'Sanskritization in Eastern Nepal'. *Ethnologogy*. 15: 63-75.

——. 1976.'Limbu Women and Economic Development in Eastern Nepal'. *Himalaya Ecologie Ethnologie 268*. Paris: CNRS.

Joshi, Bhuvan Lal and Rose, Leo E. 1966. *Democratic Innovations in Nepal: A Study in Political Acculturation*. Berkeley: University of California Press.

Joshi, Hari Ram. 1974. *Ancient Inscriptions of Nepal*. Kathmandu: The Royal Nepal Academy.

Joshi, Chadani. 1980. 'A Glimpse of Nepalese Rural Women'. *Journal of Rural Development and Social Welfare*. Volume 1, number 1, 15-27.

Joshi, Satya Mohan. 1971. *Karnali Lok Sanskrili Khanda: Ek ltihas* (Karnali folk culture: Part one history). Kathmandu: Royal Nepal Academy.

Justice, Judith. 1985. *Policies, Plans and People : Culture and Health Development in Nepal*. Berkeley: University of California Press.

Kansakar, Vidya Bir Singh. 1984. 'Indo-Nepal Migration: Problems and Prospects'. *Contributions to Nepalese Studies*. Volume 11, number 2, 49-70.

Kapp, K. William. 1963. *Hindu Culture, Economic Development and Economic Planning*. Bombay : Asia Publishing House.

Kawakita, Jiro. 1957. 'Ethno-Geographical Observations of the Nepal Himalayas' in *People of Nepal* edited by H. Kihara. Kyoto: Kyoto University Press.

——. 1974. 'The Hill Magars and their Neighbours: Hill People Surrounding the Ganges Plain'. *Synthetic Research of the Culture of the Rice Cultivation Peoples in South East Asian Countries*. Volume 3. Tokyo: Tokai University Press.

Keshar Bahadur, K. C. 1971. *The Judicial Customs of Nepal*. Kathmandu: Ratna Pustak Bhandar.

Khanal, Mohan P. 1983. *Changunarayanko Aitihasik Samagri* (Historic Materials of Changunarayan). Kathmandu: CNAS, Tribhuvan University.

Khanal, Yadu Nath. 1987. 'Reflections on Nepal-US Relations' in *Nepal: Perspectives on Development issues, Occasional Paper No. 12*. Berkeley: Center for South and Southeast Asian Studies, University of California.

Kirkpatrick, C. 1811. Reprinted 1964. *An Account of the Kingdom of Nepal*. New Delhi: Manjushri Publishing House.

Kolver, Bernhard. 1980. 'Aspects of Nepalese Culture : Ancient Inscriptions and Modern Yatras'. *Proceedings of the First Symposium of Nepal German Sanskritists 1979*. Kathmandu: Institute of Sanskrit Studies.

Kosambi, D. D. 1965. *Ancient India: A History of its Culture and Civilization*. New York: Pantheon Books.

Kumar, S. 1967. *Rana Policy in Nepal: Origin and Growth*. Bombay: Asia Publishing House.

Kuper, Leo. 1971. 'Political Changes in Plural Societies: Problems in Racial Pluralism'. *International Social Science Journal*. 23: 594-607.

Landon, P. 1928. *Nepal*. 2 vols. London: Constable.

Leach, E. R. 1966. *Rethinking Anthropology, London School of Economics Monograph on Social Anthropology*. New York: University of London, The Althone Press.

Levi, Sylvain. 1905-1908. *Le Nepal: Etude Historique un Royaune Hindou*. 3 vols. Paris: Earnest Leroux.

Levine, Nancy. 1981. 'Law, Labour and Economic Ulnerability of Women in Nynba Society'. *Kailash*. Volume 8, numbers 3 and 4, 123- 54.

1987. 'Fathers and Sons: Kinship Value and Validation in Tibetan Polyandry'. *MAN*. Volume 22, number 2, 267-87.

____ . 1987. 'Castic, State and Ethnic Boundaries in Nepal'. *Journal of Asian Studies*. Volume 46, number 1, 71-88.

Locke, John K. 1980. Karunamaya: *The Cult of Avalokiteswara-Matsyendranath in the Valley of Nepal.* Kathmandu: CNAS, Tribhuvan University.

Lohani, Govinda P. 1983. Comments on a seminar paper in *Foreign Aid and Development: Proceedings of a Seminar.* Kathmandu: IDS.

Macdonald, A. W. 1974. *Essays on the Ethnology of Nepal and South Asia.* Volume 1. Kathmandu: Ratna Pustak Bhandar.

____. 1976. 'Sorcery in the Code of 1853' in *Spirit Possessions in the Nepal Himalayas.* New Delhi : Vikas Publishing House.

Macdonald, A. W. and Stahl, Anne Vergati. 1979. *Newar Art: Nepalese Art During the Malla Period.* New Delhi: Vikas Publishing House.

Macfarlane, A. 1976. *Resources and Population: A Study of the Gurungs of Nepal.* Cambridge: Cambridge University Press.

Malla, K. P. 1973. 'The Intellectual in Nepalese Society' in *Nepal in Perspective,* edited by P. S. Rama and K. P. Malla. Kathmandu: CEDA.

____. 1981. 'Linguistic Archaelogy of the Nepal Valley. Preliminary Report'. *Kailash.* Volume 8, numbers 1 and 2, 5-23.

____. 1983. 'River-names of the Nepal Valley : A Study in Cultural Annexation'. *Contributions to Nepalase Studies.* Volume 10, numbers 1 and 2, 57-68.

____. ed. 1989. *Nepal: Perspectives on Continuity and Change.* Kathmandu: CNAS, Tribhuvan University.

Manandhar, Renuka, et al. 1982. *Balmaganteko Sambhabyata Adhyayan Prativedan* (Report of the study of child beggars). Kathmandu: Ministry of Labour and Social Welfare, HMGN.

Manandhar, Tri Ratna. 1982. 'Kaji Yukla Thup Prati Nepalle Liyeko Niti'. *Contributions to Nepalese Studies.* Volume 10, numbers 1 and 2, 117-26.

____. 1984. *Nepal-Bhot Vival (BS 1939-41).* Kathmandu: CNAS. Tribhuvan University.

____. 1985. 'Nepalko Saugat Velayatlai'. *Contributions to Nepalese Studies.* Volume 13, number 1, 95-122.

Manzardo, Andrew E. 1976. 'The Byanshi: An Ethnographic Note on a Trading Group in Far Western Nepal'. *Contributions to Nepalese Studies.* Volume 3, number 2, 84-118.

March, Kathryn. 1974. 'Of People and Naks: The Management and Meaning of High Altitude Herding Among Contemporary Solu Sherpas'. *Contributions to Nepalese Studies.* Volume 4, number 2, 63-97.

Mcdougal, Charles. 1968. *Village and Household Economy in Far Western Nepal.* Kathmandu: Tribhuvan University Press.

____. 1973. The Kulunge Rai. Kathmandu : Ratna Pustak Bhandar.

Messerschmidt, Donald T. 1976. *The Gurungs of Nepal: Conflict and Change in a Village Society.* Warminister: Aris and Phillips.

____. 1978. 'Dhikur: Rotating Credit Association in Nepal' in *Himalayan Anthropology: The Indo Tibetan Interface,* edited by J. Fisher. The Hague: Mouton.

____. 1982. 'Miteri in Nepal: Fictive Kin Ties that Bind'. Kailash. Volume 9, number 1, 5-44.

Mihaly, E. B. 1965. *Foreign Aid and Politics in Nepal : A Case Study.* London : Oxford University Press.

Mikame, Kiotomi. 1979. 'A Note on the Phaguwa Festival of Chitwan Tharu'. *Kailash.* Volume 7, numbers 3 and 4, 226-46.

Miller, Casper. S. J. 1979. *Faith-Healers in the Himalayas.* Kathmandu: CNAS, Tribhuvan University.

____ . 1990. *Decision Making in Village Nepal. Kathmandu: Sahayogi Press.*

Mills, C. Wright. 1954. *The Sociological Imagination.* London: Oxford University Press.

Ministry of Finance, HMG. 1989. *Economic Survey : Financial Year 1988-89.* Kathmandu : HMG.

Mishra, Chaitanya. 1984. 'Social Research in Nepal: A Critique and a Proposal'. *Contributions to Nepalese Studies.* Volume 11, number 2, 1-11.

___ . 1984. 'Political Economy of Population Redistribution: A Case study of a Dang Village'. *Contributions to Nepalese Studies.* Volume II, number 3, 1-10.

____ . 1987. 'Development and Underdevelopment' in *Occasional Papers in Sociology and Anthropology 1.* Kathmandu: Department of Sociology and Anthropology. Tribhuvan University.

Mishra, Chaitanya and Sharma, Pitamber. 1983. 'Foreign Aid and Social Structure: Notes on Inter-State Relationship' in *Foreign Aid and Development in Nepal: Proceedings of a Seminar.* Kathmandu : IDS.

Morgan, Edmund S. 1975. 'Working the American Land' in *We Americans,* edited by Gilbert Grosvenor. Washington: National Geographic Society.

Molnar, Augusta. 1981. 'The Kham Magar of Thabang: The Status of Women in Nepal'. Volume 2, part 2. Kathmandu : CEDA, Tribhuvan University.

Nakame, Chie. 1970. *Japanese Society.* London: Weidenfield and Nicolson.

National Planning Commission, Central Bureau of Statistics, HMG. *Population Monograph of Nepal.* Kathmandu.

Nepal, Nirish. 1982. 'A Peep into our Past'. *Rolamba.* Volume 2, number 2, 30-38 and number 3, 28-38.

Nepal, Rohit Kumar. 1978. *Dodhare ra Karikusika Dhimal Jhapa: Panchayat Training Centre.* Kathmandu.

Nepali, Chittaranjan. 1965. *General Bhimsen Thapa ra Tatkalin Nepal* (General Bhimsen Thapa and contemporary Nepal). Kathmandu: Ratna Pustak Bhandar.

Nepali, Gopal Sung. 1965. *The Newars: An Ethno-Sociological Study of a Himalayan Community*. Bombay: United Asia Publications.

Nepal Rastra Bank. 1988. *Multipurpose Household Budget Survey: A Study of Income Distribution, Employment and Consumption Patterns in Nepal*. Kathmandu.

Oppitz, Michacl. 1974. 'Myths and Facts: Reconsidering some Data Concerning the Clan History of the Sherpas'. *Kailash*. Volume 2, number 1 and 2, 121-32.

Ortner, Sherry B. 1978. *Sherpas Through their Rituals*, Cambridge: Cambridge University Press.

Pandey, Bhim Bahadur. 1982. *Tyas Bakhatko Nepal* (Nepal of that Period). 2 volumes. Kathmandu : CNAS, Tribhuvan University.

Pandey, Devendra Raj. 1983. 'Foreign Aid in Nepal's Development, an Overview' in *Foreign Aid and Development in Nepal: Proceedings of a Seminar*. Kathmandu : IDS.

Pandey, Madhav Raj. 1973. 'How Jang Bahadur Established Rana Rule in Nepal'. *Contributions to Nepalese Studies*. Volume 1, number 1, 50-63.

Pandey, Ram Nivas. 1985. 'Archaeological Remains of Lumbini : The Birthplace of Lord Buddha'. *Contributions to Nepalese Studies*. Volume 12, number 3, 51-62.

Pant, Dinesh Raj. 1964. 'Nepal Rajyako Ekikaranko Falasworup Bidwanharuko Dristikon Arko Autar'. *Purnima*. Volume 1, number 2, 33-38.

_____ . 1973. 'Ram Shahko Rajyakal'. *Kailash*. Volume 1, number 1, 76-79.

Pant, Naya Raj. 1964. 'Sthiti Malla Tatha Jatpat'. *Purnima*. Volume 1, number 2. 1-10.

_____ . 1968. *Shri Panch Prithvinarayan Shahko Upadesh*. 4 volumes. Patan: Jagadamba Prakashan.

Pant, Thakur Nath. 1983. 'Foreign Aid and Agricultural Development in Nepal' in *Foreign Aid and Development in Nepal: Proceedings of a Seminar*. Kathmandu: IDS.

Pant, Yadav Prasad. 1969. *Planning for Prosperity: A Study in Nepal's Experiences*. 3rd edition. Kathmandu : Sahayogi.

Petech, Luciano. 1984. *Medieval History of Nepal (750-1480)*. 2nd Revised Edition. *ISMEO Serie Orientale ROMA 54*. Roma.

Peters, L. 1979. 'Shamanism and Medicine in Developing Nepal'. *Contributions to Nepalese Studies*. Volume 6, number 2, 27-43.

Pignede, B. 1966. *Les Gurungs: Une Populations Himalayenne du Nepal*. The Hague and Paris: Mouton.

Poffenberger, Mark. 1980. *Patterns of Change in the Nepal Himalaya*. Delhi: Macmillan.

Pokhrel, Balkrishna. ed. 1974. *Pancsaya Varsa*. Kathmandu: Sajha Prakashan.

Poudyal, Madhav P. 1984. *Public Administration and Nation Building in Nepal*. Delhi: NBO Publishers

Pradhan, Bina. 1981. *The Newar Women of Bulu : The Status of Women in Nepal*. Volume 2, part 6. Kathmandu: CEDA, Tribhuvan University.

Pradhan, Bina and Shrestha, Indira. 1983. 'Foreign Aid and Women'. *Foreign Aid and Development in Nepal: Proceedings of a Seminar*. Kathmandu: IDS.

Pradhan, Prachanda. 1976. *Public Administration in Nepal*. Kathmandu: Tribhuvan University.

Pradhan, Rukmini Onta. 1985. 'Vikramsila Mahaviharako Aitihasik Mahattwo'. *Contributions to Nepalese Studies*. Volume 12, number 2, 103-110.

Radha Krishna, J. 1987. *Brahmans of India*. Allahabad: Chugh Publications.

Rai, Navin Kumar. 1973. 'Khamba: Ek Ardha Bhramanshil Jaati'. *Contributions to Nepalese Studies.* Volume 1, number 1, 64-75

___ . 1985. *People of the Stones: The Chepangs of Central Nepal.* Kathmandu: CNAS, Tribhuvan University.

Rajaure, Dron. 1981. *The Tharu Women of Sukhrawar: The Status of Women in Nepal.* Volume 2, part 3. Kathmandu: CEDA, Tribhuvan University.

Rauber, Hanna. 1980. 'The Humli Khyampas of Far Western Nepal: A Study in Ethnogenesis'. *Contributions to Nepalese Studies.* Volume 8, number 1, 57-80.

Regmi, D.R. 1958. *A Century of Family Autocracy in Nepal, 1946-1949.* 2nd edition. Kathmandu: The Nepali Congress.

___ . 1961. *Modern Nepal.* Calcutta. Firma K.L.M.

___ . 1965-66. *Medieval Nepal,* Parts 1 and 2. Calcutta: Firma K.L.M.

Regmi, Mahesh Chandra. 1971. *A Study in Nepali Economic History: 1768-1846.* New Delhi: Manjushri Publishing House.

___ . 1978. *Thatched Huts and Stucco Palaces: Peasants and Landlords in 19th Century Nepal.* New Delhi: Vikas Publishing House.

Reinhard, Johan. 1976. 'The Banrajas—A Vanishing Himalayan Tribe'. *Contributions to Nepalese Studies.* Volume 4, number 1, 1- 22.

Reischauer, Edwin O. 1978. *The Japanese.* Cambridge and London: Harvard University Press.

___ . 1981. *Japan: The Story of a Nation.* New York: Alfred A Knopf.

Rhee, Kyu Ho. 1983. *Struggle for National Identity in the Third World.* New Jersey and Seoul: Hollym International Corporation.

Riccardi, Theodore Jr. 1975. 'An Account of Nepal from the Vir Vinod of Shyamaldas'. *Kailash*. Volume 3, number 3, 199-286.

___. 1977. 'The Royal Edicts of King Rama Shah of Gorkha'. *Kailash*. Volume 5, number 1, 29-66.

Rose, Leo E. and Fisher, M. 1970. *The Politics of Nepal: Persistence and Change in an Asian Monarchy*: Ithaca: Cornell University Press.

Rose, Leo E and Scholz, John. 1980. Nepal: *Profile of a Himalayan Kingdom*. Colorado: Westview Press.

Ross, J. L. 1982. 'Adaptations to a Changing Salt Trade: The View from Humla'. *Contributions to Nepalese Studies*. Volume 10, numbers 1 and 2, 43-50.

Rosser, Collin. 1966. 'Social Mobility in Newar Caste System' in *Caste and Kin in Nepal, India and Ceylon*, edited by C. Von Furer-Haimendorf. Bombay: Asia Publishing House.

Sahlins, Marshall. 1976. *Culture and Practical Reason*. Chicago: Chicago University Press.

Sanwal, B.D. 1965. *Nepal and the East India Company*. London: Asia Publishing House.

Schloss, Aran. 1983. *The Politics of Development : Transportation Policy in Nepal*. Berkeley: UC Press.

Schroeder, Robert and Schroeder, Elaine. 1979. 'Women in Nepali Agriculture: All Work and No Power'. *The Journal of Development and Administration Studies*. Volume 1, number 2, 178-92.

Schuler, Sydney. 1977. 'Migratory Traders of Baragaon'. *Contributions to Nepalese Studies*. 5: 71-84.

____. 1981. *The Women of Baragaon: The Status of Women in Nepal*. Volume 2, part 5. Kathmandu: CEDA, Tribhuvan University.

Schumacher, E. F. 1973. *Small is Beautiful: Economics as if People Mattered*. London: Blond and Briggs.

Seddon, David 1987. *Nepal: A State of Poverty*. New Delhi: Vikas Publishing House.

Sen, Jahar. 1973. 'Slave Trade on the Indo-Nepal Border in the Nineteenth Century'. *Kailash*. Volumes 1 and 2: 159-67.

___ . 1977. *India Nepal Trade in the Nineteenth Century*. Calcutta: Firma K. L. M.

Shah, Rishikesh. 1981. 'Sources of Ancient and Medieval Nepal.' *Rolamba*. Volume 1, number 4, 3-10.

___ . 1982. 'Social Conditions in Medieval Nepal.' *Rolamba*. Volume 2, number 4, 3-9.

Sharma, Janak Lal. 1982. *Hamro Samaj: Ek Adhyayan* (A study of our society). Kathmandu: Sajha Prakashan.

Sharma, Prayag Raj. 1971. 'The Matwali Chhetris of Western Nepal'. *Himalayan Review*. 4: 43-60

___ . 1971. *Paschim Nepalko Himalayama Pujine Kehi Deutaharu tatha Tes Bhekko Dharmik Rupko Euta Samannya Charcha* (An elementary discussion on certain deities being worshipped in the West Nepal Himalayas and the religious form of that region). Karnali Pradesh: Ek Bito Adhyayan.

___ . 1977. 'Caste Social Mobility and Sanskritization: A Study of Nepal's Old Legal Code'. *Kailash*. Volume 5, number 4, 277-300.

___ . 1983. 'Nepal Culture ..d Society: A Historic Perspective'. *Contributions to Nepalese Studies*. 10: 1-2.

___ . 1986. 'Ethnicity and National Integration in Nepal: A Statement of the Problem'. *Contributions to Nepalese Studies*. Volume 13, number 2, 129-36.

Sharma, Som Nath. trans. 1967. *Kautillyako Artha Shastra*. Kathmandu: Royal Nepal Academy.

Shepherd, Gary. 1982. *Life Among Magars*. Kathmandu Sahayogi Prakashan.

Shrestha, Bihari Krishna. 1976. *Karnali Lok Sanskriti, Janajivan: Diyargaunka Thakuriharu*. Volume 3. Kathmandu: Royal Nepal Academy.

___. 1983. 'Technical Assistance and the Growth of Administrative Capacity in Nepal' in *Foreign Aid and Development in Nepal: Proceedings of a Seminar*. Kathmandu: IDS.

Shrestha, B.P. 1967. *The Economy of Nepal*. Bombay: Vohra & Co Publishers.

Shrestha, H.B. 1985. 'Pattern of Urban and Rural Growth of Population in Nepal'. *Contributions to Nepalese Studies*. Volume 3, number 2, 11-18.

Shrestha, Tek Bahadur. 1981. 'Kirti Bam Malla ra Uska Aprakasit Abhilekh'. *Contributions to Nepalese Studies*. Volume 3, number 2, 97-134.

___. 1983. 'Gulmi Rajyako Rajnaitik Itihas ra Kehi Aprakasit Aitihasik Samagri'. *Contributions to Nepalese Studies*. Volume 11, number 1, 101-13.

Shrestha, Madan Krishna. 1984. 'Nepali Samajma Gopali Ek Parichaya'. *Ancient Nepal*. 79: 9-12.

Shrivastava. 1958. *The Tharus: A Study in Cultural Dynamics*. Agra: Agra University Press.

Singh, Bhagirath. 1984. *Kusbadhiyaharuko Parichayatmek Adhyayan*. Nepalgunj: Panchayat Development Training Centre.

Singh, Ganesh Man. 1988. An Interview to *Satahik Bimarsha*, 10 October 1988.

Singh, L.P. 1983. *Morality in Public Affairs*. New Delhi: Centre for Policy Research.

Slusser, Mary Shepherd, 1982. *Nepal Mandala: A Cultural Study of the Kathmandu Valley*. 2 volumes. Princeton: Princeton University Press.

Snellgrove, David L. 1961. *Himalayan Pilgrimage*. Oxford: Bruno Cassirer.

___ . 1967. *Four Lamas of Dolpo*. Oxford: Bruno Cassirer.

___ . 1975. *Buddhist Himalaya*. Oxford: Bruno Cassirer.

Soedhatmoko. 1986. 'Values in Transition'. *The Washington Quarterly*. Volume 9, number 4.

Somlai, Ivan Victor. 1982. Two Twelve-Year Festivals in the Thak Khola'. *Kailash*. Volume 9, numbers 2 and 3, 159-76.

Srinivas, M.N. 1969. *Social Change in Modern India*. Berkeley: University of California Press.

Stein, R. A. 1972. *Tibetan Civilization*. Stanford: Stanford University Press.

Stiller. L. F. 1968. *Prithvinarayan Shah in the Light of Dibya Updesh*. Bihar: Catholic Press.

___ . 1975. *The Rise of House of Gorkha*. Patna: Patna Jesuit Society.

___ . 1976. *The Silent Cry: The People of Nepal 1816-1839*. Kathmandu: Sahyogi Prakashan.

___ . 1981. *Letters from Kathmandu: The Kot Massacre*. Kathmandu: CNAS, Tribhuvan University.

Stiller L. F. and Yadav. 1979. *Planning for People*. Kathmandu: CNAS, Tribhuvan University.

Stone, Linda, 1978. 'Food Symbolism in Hindu Nepal'. *Contributions to Nepalese Studies*. Volume 3, number 3, 55-80.

Strickland, S. S. 1984. 'Resources and Population Among the Gurungs: 1958-1980'. *Kailash*. Volume 11, numbers 3 and 4, 211-54.

Tewari, Ranjit, et al. 1964. *Aitihasik Patra Sangraha*. Part 2. Kathmandu: Nepal Sanskritik Parishad.

Thapaliya, Bhojraj. 1987. *Chepang Jati Ek Parichaya* Sunsari: Nepal.

Toba, Ingrid. 1977. 'Folk Arts and Culture: Change as Observed in a Khaling Village'. *Kailash*. Volume 5, number 1, 13-28.

Toba, Sueyosi. 1975. 'Plant Names in Khaling: A Study in Ethnobotany and Village Economy'. *Kailash*. Volume 3, number 2, 145-70.

Tocqueville, Alexis. 1954. Reprint. *Democracy in America*. 2 volumes. New York: Alfred E Knopf, Vintage Books.

Toffin, Gerhard. 1976. 'Le si ka bhoey, Festin de la tete, chez les Newar, Newar jatile manaune sika bhoey.' *Kailash*. Volume 4, number 4, 329-38.

Tucci, Guiseppe. 1956. *Preliminary Report on Two Scientific Expeditions on Nepal*. Volume 9, Roma: ISMEO.

——. 1962. *Nepal: The Discovery of the Malla*. London: Allen and Unwin.

——. 1973. *Transhimalaya*. London: Basil and Jenkin.

Tuladhar, J. M., Gubhaju, B. B. and Stoeckel, J. 1977. *The Population of Nepal: Structure and Change*. Berkeley: CSSAS, UC.

Upadhyaya, Kiran D. 1984,. 'Educational Aspirations and Expectations of Rural Youths in Rautahat District of Nepal'. *Contributions to Nepalese Studies*. Volume 11, number 2, 37-48.

Uprety, B. P. 1976. 'Limbuwan Today : Process and Problems'. *Contributions to Nepalese Studies*. Volume 3, number 2, 47-70.

Vajracharya, Dhanavajra. 1988. 'Licchavi Kalko Itihasma Kiratkalko Prabhav' (Influence of Kirat Period on the Lichhavi Period). *Purnima*. Volume 17, number 5, 1.

——. ed. 1972. *Baburam Acharya ra Unka* Kriti (Baburam Acharya and his Works). Kathmandu: CNAS, Tribhuvan University.

——. 1980. 'Madhyakalik Nepalka ek Prakhyat Raja Shiva Dev' (Shiva Dev, a famous king of the Medieval Period). *Contributions to Nepalese Studies*. Volume 8, number 1, 207-22.

Vajracharya, D, and Shrestha, T. B. 1974. Dolkhako Aithasik Ruprekha (Historic outline of Dolkha). Kathmandu: CNAS, Tribhuvan University.

___. 1975. Nuwakotko Aitihasik Ruprekha (Historic outline of Nuwakot). Kathmandu: CNAS, Tribhuvan University.

___. 1978. *Panchali Sashan Padhhatiko Aitihasik Vivechana* (Historic analysis of the Panchayat administration during Lichhavi Period). Kathmandu: CNAS, Tribhuvan University.

Vajracharya, D. and Malla, K. P. 1985. *The Gopal Rajavamsavali. Nepal Research Centre Publication No. 9*. Kathmandu: Franz Sterner Vernag Wiesbaden GMBH.

Vinding, Michiel. 1978. 'The Local Oral Tradition about the Kingdom of Thin Garab Dzong'. *Kailash*. Volume 6, number 3, 181-94.

Weber, Max. 1977. *The Theory of Social and Economic Organization With an Introduction by Talcott Parson*. New York: Charles Scribner's Sons.

___. 1958. *The Protestant Ethic and the Spirit of Capitalism*, translated by Talcott Parson. New York: Charles Scribner's Sons.

Weil, Leon J. 1987. *The Private Sector in Nepal: An Ambassador's Views*. An address delivered to the Rotary Club in Kathmandu. Memeograph.

Whelpton, John. 1987. 'The Ancestors of Jang Bahadur Rana : History, Propaganda and Legend.' *Contributions to Nepalese Studies*. Volume 14, number 3, 161-92.

Wolf, Eric R. 1982. *Europe and the People Without History*. Berkeley: UC Press

World Bank (The). *World Development Report 1989: Financial Systems and Development, World Development Indicators*. The World Bank: Oxford University Press.

Yatri, Purna Prakash Nepal. 1983. *Raute Lokjivan* (Raute Folklife). Kathmandu: Development of Publicity, HMG.

Yogi, Narahari Nath. 1955. *Itihas Prakas*. Volumes 1 and volume 2, parts 1, 2 and 3. Kathmandu: Itihas Prakas Mandal.

____. 1965. *Itihas Prakasana Sandhipatra Sangraha* (Collection of Treaty Papers). Part 1. Benaras: Yogi Naraharinath.